- ●   Large settlements mentioned in Essay & Tables
- •   Small settlements mentioned in Essay & Tables
- △   Other large settlements
- ▵   Other small settle
- ———   Known roads
- — — —   Conjectural roads
-    Standing water an
- Extent of fen

N

₃

ll

△Thetford

●BURY ST. EDMUNDS

0   5   10 Miles

) Part of pre-drainage East Anglia showing places mentioned in the documents. Based on *Regiones Inundatae*, 1648.

DOWNHAM-IN-THE-ISLE

*A Study of an Ecclesiastical Manor
in the Thirteenth and Fourteenth Centuries*

TO THE MEMORY OF MY PARENTS

DOWNHAM-IN-THE-ISLE

*A Study of an Ecclesiastical Manor
in the Thirteenth and Fourteenth Centuries*

M. CLARE COLEMAN

THE BOYDELL PRESS

© M. Clare Coleman 1984

Published by The Boydell Press
an imprint of Boydell & Brewer Ltd
PO Box 9 Woodbridge Suffolk IP12 3DF

ISBN 0 85115 401 8

Coleman, M. Clare
  Downham-in-the-Isle.
  1. Downham-in-the-Isle (Cambridgeshire and Ely)
  —History—Sources
  I. Title
  942.6'53   DA690.D/

  ISBN 0-85115-401-8

Printed by Nene Litho
Bound by Woolnough Bookbinding
Both of Wellingborough, Northants.

CONTENTS

LIST OF TABLES

LIST OF MAPS AND ILLUSTRATIONS

Acknowledgments

If I were to say all that I would like to say about the many people who have given me advice, help and encouragement over this study of Downham-in-the-Isle these acknowledgments would be almost as long as the study itself – not half of them can be mentioned: but I am especially grateful to the following:

Those who have helped me with the transcription and translation of the documents, R.C. Smail and Peter Linehan, both of whom read (and improved) much of my work: Dorothy Owen, who led me to the Downham documents in the first place, and Dorothea Oschinsky, both of whom read for me many portions of the rolls under the ultraviolet lamp.

Martin Stephenson, Richard Smith and Jack Ravensdale for their advice, respectively, on mediaeval farming and on the demography and the mediaeval plan of the village.

Karen Pearson for her great kindness and skill in making (in her home in Alaska) the superb plan and maps; Andrew Cook for advice and help over the mapping instructions and Kyllikki Pekola for her clever additions to Map 3.

Simon Lamb, Leonore Hoke and the Cambridge University Library for their excellent photographs.

The staffs of the Manuscript Room and the Map Room of the Cambridge University Library for tolerating me and giving me so much willing help.

Dorothy Lukyn-Williams, who has nobly and patiently typed my original, amended and entirely re-written scripts, giving helpful advice throughout on many points of detail.

Christine Linehan, who has edited the script and given invaluable constructive help and criticism throughout.

Dr Edward Miller, who gave time to read what I thought was my final script and with his wisdom and deep knowledge of the history of the Isle, rescued me from more than one pitfall and helped me to see the pattern of the events of mediaeval Downham.

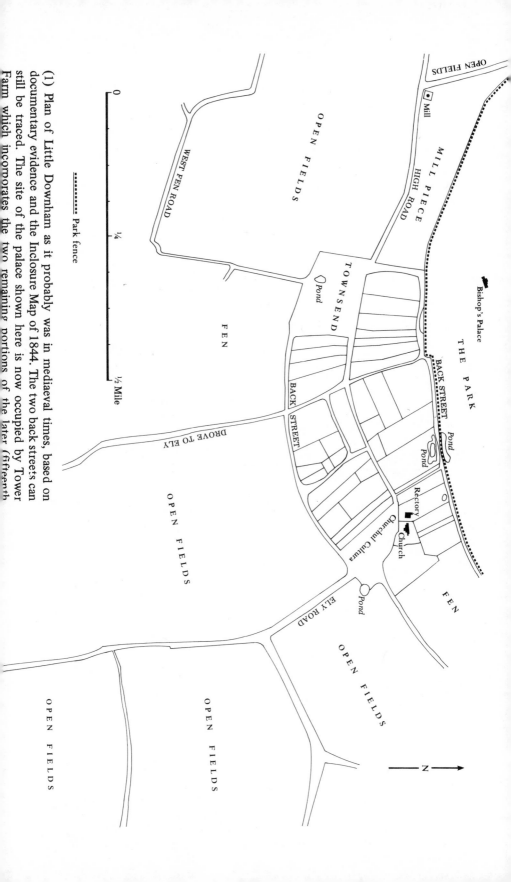

(1) Plan of Little Downham as it probably was in mediaeval times, based on documentary evidence and the Inclosure Map of 1844. The two back streets can still be traced. The site of the palace shown here is now occupied by Tower Farm which incorporates the two remaining portions of the later (fifteenth

·········· Park fence

0   ¼   ½ Mile

OPEN FIELDS

WEST FEN ROAD

FEN

TOWNSEND

Pond

BACK STREET

DROVE TO ELY

OPEN FIELDS

BACK STREET

Pond

Pond

Rectory

Churchul Culture

Church

Pond

ELY ROAD

OPEN FIELDS

OPEN FIELDS

OPEN FIELDS

OPEN FIELDS

FEN

N

Bishop's Palace

THE PARK

MILL PIECE

HIGH ROAD

Mill

OPEN FIELDS

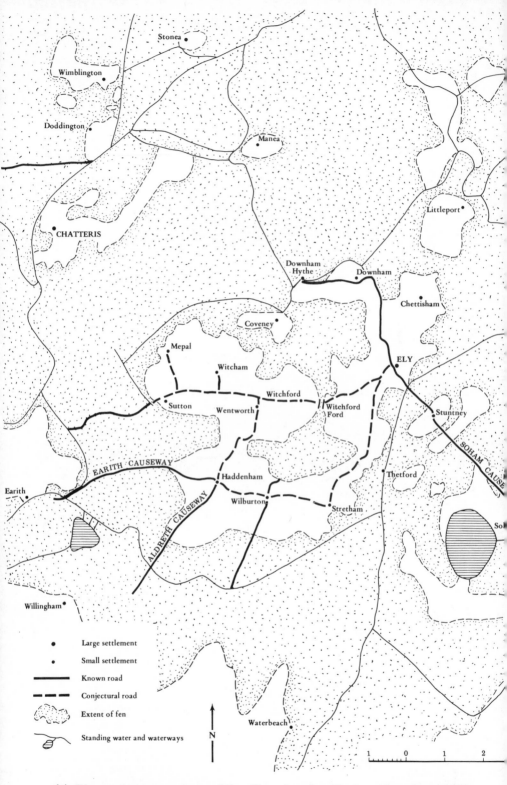

(2) The pre-drainage environs of the village, based on *Regiones Inundatae*, 1648. Downham shared an island with nine other villages and Ely, and communication beyond this was by water or by one of the three causeways, Soham, Erith and Aldreth. It was on the Aldreth causeway that the tenants of Downham did some of their customary work.

INTRODUCTION

This study concerns the village of Little Downham, or Downham-in-the-Isle, which lies 2½ miles north-west of Ely. The period of the study is from 1222, the year of an early survey, to 1377 – practically the reigns of Henry III and the first three Edwards.

The history of the village is set against a national tapestry dominated by revolt, wars and plague – the very great discontent of Henry's reign resulting in the Barons' Revolt;[1] the thirty years of war with Scotland with its raids deep into the northern counties; the Hundred Years' War with France with the glorious early phase of Crécy and Poitiers followed by the decline due to plague and exhaustion among the troops; and finally the devastation caused by the Black Death in 1349/50 and its recurrence in 1360/62.

The documents used are:

The Extent of 1222: B.M. Cott. M.S. Tiberius BII
The Extent of 1251: Ely Diocesan Records G 3/27
The Court Roll of Edward II: E.D.R. C 11/1
The Court Roll of Edward III: E.D.R. C 11/2
The Downham Reeve's Accounts for these reigns: E.D.R. D 10/2/1-27
The Wisbech Barton Reeve's Stock Accounts: E.D.R. D 8/1/3, 11, 17, 18;
    D 8/2/13, 17-19, 23-25

They are all written in mediaeval Latin, on parchment, the extents in book-hand, the court rolls and accounts in court-hand. Each of the extents is bound in a volume with similar contemporary surveys of the bishop's other manors. The court rolls and accounts are written on membranes about 10 inches wide and 2½ to 7 feet long, the length sometimes being increased by another membrane being sewn to the foot of the first.

The Extent of 1222 was ordered by Bishop John of Fountains, Bishop of Ely from 1220 to 1225. It describes the demesne, giving acreages of arable land and meadow and mentions one fishery. It gives lists of the free tenants and the tofters, and records the rents and the slight duties which they owed to the lord. It gives lists of the customary tenants (holders of full lands and half lands) and

---

1 The Isle was in sympathy with the rebels. On 5 March 1267 the king ordered that 'strong and approved men' from the towns of the Norfolk and Suffolk shore should 'come to Lynn and go against the Isle of Ely with barges and men armed . . . to aggrieve the king's enemies in that Isle' and amerce and punish them 'without peril of life or limb'. If the rebels did not submit to justice the king would 'punish them as their rebellion and perversity' required. (*Calendar of Patent Rolls*: 1266-72, p. 44)

of the cottagers (holders of cotlands) and records the many services they could be called upon to do and the various dues which they had to pay.

The Extent of 1251 was ordered by Bishop Hugh of Northwold, Bishop of Ely from 1229 to 1254. The original survey is no longer in existence but there are three copies, all made one or two hundred years later. The one used for this study is contained, with those for his forty-nine other manors, in the Old Ely Coucher Book. The other copies are in the library of Gonville & Caius College, Cambridge (MS. 485/489) and in the British Library (MS. Cotton Claudius Cl 1). This extent is very much longer than that of 1222, describing the demesne in greater detail and giving more precisely the duties and obligations arising out of the holdings.

The Court Roll of Edward II consists of ten membranes: ten others are missing. There is no membrane until that for 1310/11. The year 1312/13 is missing and there is a six-year gap from 1316/17 to 1321/22 (Table I).

The Court Roll of Edward III consists of twenty-eight membranes: thirty years are missing, the twenty-six from 1335/36 to 1360/61 and four later years, 1366/67, 1370/71, 1371/72 and 1374/75 (Table II).

The Reeve's Accounts are the accounts of the demesne: every membrane, each a separate roll, contains a year's accounts from Michaelmas to Michaelmas (except when, on a change of lordship, only part of a year is dealt with). Every membrane has, in effect, four separate accounts. The financial accounts, first the credits, then the expenses, occupy the recto: on the dorso are, first, the grain account, then the stock account and lastly the *opera* account. The grain account deals separately with every sort of crop, showing, in quarters and bushels, how much was produced from the harvest of the previous year, how much was bought or obtained from other manors, how much sown over how many acres at how many bushels an acre, and how much disposed of in liveries to servants or otherwise. The stock account deals in the same wealth of detail with every sort of animal in the demesne, from the stallion in the stable to the doves in the dovecot. The *opera* account sets out how many works were due to the lord, how the credits were earned by the tenants and (entered as 'works sold') how many unearned credits were paid for by them.

Except for the account for part of 1301/02, there are none until that for 1318/19. Thereafter there are twenty-seven membranes: thirty-one are missing, the longest gaps being one of nine years, one of five and two of four years (Table III).

The twenty-six year gap in the court roll of Edward III divides it into two distinct series, one dealing with a period of prosperity and rising population when the land was being used to its utmost limits, the other reporting the times after two visitations of the Black Death.

The reeve's stock accounts between 1346 and 1352, recording the beasts received as heriot (death duty) show that during the plague years this duty was paid for over half of the customary tenants (Table X). To guess at the total number of deaths caused by the plague in the village one should probably add a greater proportion of cottagers and landless people.

There would be depopulation, too, caused by villagers absconding in search of higher wages. By 1362 there were many vacant holdings: also, only a small part of the demesne was being cultivated by the lord (for lack of labour) and only a small acreage of it was being let (for lack of tenants). So, much land was returning to waste. In fact, the conditions after 'the gap' were so different from those in the earlier years that the two series had to be taken separately whenever statistics were considered.

I. THE PLACE

Like all fen villages, Little Downham stands on rising ground, the village itself being above the fifty-foot contour line, and a strip running west from the village for over a mile being above the twenty-foot contour. It is a street-plan village: the main street, half a mile long, runs roughly north-east to south-west, from the fourteenth century church at the north-east end to the part of the village known as Townsend at the other.

The village of the fourteenth century will have followed much of the present form, the church at one end and Townsend at the other. It stretched to Townsend at any rate by 1362 when one Simon atte Townesend appears in the court roll as a juror. The main street, then known as the king's highway, figures frequently in the rolls as an illicit depository for the villagers' dung-heaps. The back streets that ran behind the crofts on either side of the highway can still be traced.

Around the village lay three open fields, West Field, East Field and a field called variously Parrocesone (1222 extent), Aggrene (1251 extent) and Le Parrok (Reeve's accounts 1319/20, etc.). The rent roll of 1369/70 (Appendix I) and the court roll of 1 December 1373 (Appendix II) show the fields further divided into *culturae*. In the fields lay, in strips, the arable lands of the demesne and those of the villeins and the free tenants, altogether a little over nine hundred 'nominal' or customary acres. The Inclosure map of 1844 shows the fields stretching westwards from the village in a tongue of land over a mile long and less than half a mile wide – the strip over the twenty-foot contour line. The rest of the fields lay mainly to the south-east of the village in a roughly square block (also twenty feet above sea level), bisected by the Ely Road. No fields are shown to the north of the village and here lay the lord's park of 250 acres (1251 extent) containing some woodland, some grazing and some private fen, the home of pheasants and rabbits and the 'beasts of the chase', the fallow deer: north of the park lay the common fen. The Jonas Moore map of the Great Level of the Fens, surveyed in 1684-5, shows a great fence between three sides of the park and the fields, and a dyke separating the park from the fen on the fourth side. Within the park stood the manor house of the lord, the palace of the bishop of Ely. This was rebuilt by Bishop Alcock at the end of the fifteenth century and fell into disrepair by the beginning of the seventeenth; the two remaining portions of it are now incorporated into the buildings of Tower Farm (Park Farm on the Inclosure map) which stands on the site.

Beyond the western end of the fields, about a mile and a half from the village, was a navigable waterway, now filled with hawthorn and other vegetation, which can be seen from the Coveney Road going towards Coveney in one direction and towards Downham Hythe in the other and thence north towards Manea. It is not known when this lode was made: it was presumably a local work undertaken by the bishop just as other lodes were being dug by various monastic houses. The 1222 extent does not mention journeys by water whereas the 1251 extent specifically orders water journeys from Downham to Manea and to Chatteris and to Doddington, where the bishop had another manor house. It seems likely, therefore, that the lode was made at some time between 1222 and 1251. It must have taken a considerable amount of traffic until its waters were robbed by the larger drainage systems of two or more centuries later. The 'works' accounts contain many references to boat journeys from Downham Hythe: in 1326/27 and again in 1361/62 men were taken to repair a dam at Doddington; in 1330/31 the bishop's brother, John de l'Isle, and his sister, were taken 'on several occasions' to Doddington and Chatteris. The lode was also used for fishing: the 1251 extent refers to two fisheries, one 'at Downham Hythe which extends from Coveney Bridge to Godrigshythe' and the other, held by Ralph of Manea, 'extending from Godricshythe to Cokes lode'.

It seems that it must have been here, beside the lode, that the river meadows lay. It is obvious, from the references in the rolls, that they lay parallel to each other along the water-side: in 1368 the court records the taking up of one river meadow between those of William Hayte and Richard Bridge, the taking up of another between those of William Hayte and Nicholas the son of Simon, and another between those of William Shepherd and Katherine Cardinal. This would by lush, valuable, meadow land. Some of it, presumably, was the fifteen-acre piece 'in Holm'[1] referred to in the 1251 extent as part of the demesne. Other demesne meadow lands listed in that extent were 'in Westmead 13 acres' and 'in Aggrene, 17 acres'. That in Aggrene must have been between the arable land to the south or east of the village and the surrounding fen for beside it were 'six acres of fen which could be cleared of tussocks', thus bringing the acreage up to twenty-three.

For grazing land and meadow there was, for all the tenants, for 'the whole vill of Downham, the greater and the lesser folk', commoning on the fen, and the 1251 extent sets out exactly which parts of the fen are included, all for grazing and, with one exception, all for mowing: 'they must common on the great bank of Church Fen but it must not be mown'. There was also, of course, the common grazing on the stubble after harvest.

A feature of the village was the mill, to which all the villeins who owed 'suit of mill' had to bring their corn for grinding. It stood to the north-west of the village, not far from the palace, 'a windmill, newly made' in 1251.

---

1 E. Ekwall, in *The Concise Oxford Dictionary of English Place Names* (4th edn. Oxford, 1960) defines 'holm' as a piece of dry land in a fen.

Somewhere near the palace was a dovecot which provided a contribution to the lord's larder. This was either built or much repaired in 1343 as its expenses for labour, wood, sedges and turves in that year amounted to the considerable sum of £5. 0s. 8d.

(1) Carved head, in the Octagon of Ely Cathedral, of Bishop John of Hotham, bishop of Ely 1316–1337. The building of the Octagon and of the Lady Chapel was begun during his episcopacy. He travelled widely 'on the king's service' and was much beloved and respected by Edward III. (See Appendix III.)

Photo: Simon Lamb

(2) Extract from the Reeve's Account Roll for the year 1319/20, showing the expenses of the plough teams and the carting. One item in each case is the cost of horse-shoes: those for the plough horses (stots) were only a half-penny each,

II. THE LORD AND HIS PEOPLE

Some attempt has been made to ascertain the size and 'texture' of the population of Downham, its social and economic strata and the presence of trades other than those linked with agriculture and stock-breeding. First of all, the numbers: the 1251 extent lists 4 free tenants, 55 customary tenants and cottagers and 7 tofters: this gives 66 householders with some land. To these must be added the landless villagers — the servants at the hall and those employed by other tenants; there would also be a little group around Downham Hythe picking up a casual living out of the water transport. Some help is obtained from the court rolls: in those of the earlier series there are references to about 250 people; in those of the later series over 150 are mentioned, very few of whom are also named in the earlier rolls. In many cases these figures include two or more members of a family; on the other hand they exclude those villagers (and there must have been many) who were never entered in the roll in any capacity — as juror, as litigant or as a person dealing in land. One might hazard a guess that up to the end of the first series there were 400—500 inhabitants: there were many fewer in the later years.

The villeins of Downham were by no means all of one status. The standard holding in the open fields was a full land, fourteen 'nominal' acres, and in 1251 eight men held full lands and 24 held half lands. Some of these rented assarted land in the fen — Geoffrey the reeve, a full-lander, had 12 acres there. Later, the rolls reveal that some villagers managed to buy holdings from others; one (Geoffrey Cardinal) even acquired two full lands and a half, and many of them bought assarted land and also land from some free men. Other villagers went in extensively for sheep: some excelled in trading. These successful men became comparatively well off and they formed the aristocracy of the villeinage, taking a large part in administration. Some left wills when they died. These big families were the Cardinals, the Kedes, the Popes and the Stoneyes and (though they were cottagers) the Buks and the Scuts who were sheep farmers. The Lovechilds were a family of the later years: William was a customary tenant and a responsible member of the community. The cottagers were lower down in the social scale, with holdings of only one acre in the fields, though many of them also acquired additional lands.

As to the trades and occupations of the villagers, there is circumstantial evidence of a few. For instance, the extent of 1251 refers to the smith, Jocelyn, a cottager who paid for his holding by doing all the ironwork needed on the lord's ploughs, and also the carpenter, Warin, who, as a customary tenant, had a

7

similar arrangement in connection with the woodwork for the ploughs. The rolls show a succession of millers taking up the farm of the mill for one year. Then there were the bakers: Alan le Baxter is mentioned in December 1313 and December 1314 and seven other bakers were presented at various times for selling loaves of insufficient weight or of poor quality, Robert Hasteler with his wife and sister-in-law between 1315 and 1324, Alice Morris between 1324 and 1334, Christina Sweyn in 1326 and John de Bredenham and Robert the smith in 1328 (Table IV). In the later series of rolls there is record of a bakery in the village: Stephen Frost rented it from Robert Rote for six years at 40d. a year (2 May 1365). As no other bakers are mentioned in the later series it may be that the villagers made their own bread and took it to the bakehouse to be baked.

Some brewers and alewives, like the bakers, helpfully, sometimes regularly, broke the assize (Tables V and VI). Scattered over the twenty-five years of the earlier series of rolls, there were 70 defaulting brewers, the greatest number at any one time being 16. One brewer, Beatrice Buk, appears 15 times. It is impossible to say whether only a few did regular brewing and the others did it when they felt like it or whether quite a lot of them brewed regularly but managed to keep the right side of the law. The defaulting alewives numbered 18 in those twenty-five years, the greatest number in any one year (1310) being five.

After 1362 the picture is very different (Table VII): there were only 26 brewers, 5 of whom were sometimes presented as alewives: besides these there were only two alewives. The ratio between the population and the brewers and alewives may well have been the same as before, so many villagers having left the village or died.

Any further evidence of the existence of trades other than those connected with farming must be gleaned from trade 'surnames'. This evidence, if taken from names in the extents of 1222 and 1251, is reliable; but taken from names in the second series of court rolls (after 1360) it is far from trustworthy for by that time it was frequently the case that a man bore his father's trade surname even if he was not following his father's trade and the trade surname had thus become an inherited name, a 'real' surname. A trade name of the early fourteenth century can, with caution, be accepted as indicative of the trade of the bearer and the court rolls for the years 1310–1327 have been chosen for examination. In these years there were, according to the 'surnames':

4 smiths (but only 3 working concurrently)
7 carpenters (2 concurrent)
4 wrights (2 concurrent)
2 carters
1 miller (that is, one at a time)
1 baker (Alan le Baxter)
2 cooks (Peter Cok and John Cok)

1 sauce maker (Simon Sauser)
1 arrowmaker (Richard le Flecher)
1 cobbler (Adam le Souter)
1 cooper (Robert Cuper)
1 merchant (Hugo le Mercator)
1 barber (Walter le Barbour)
and a chamberlain (Ralph)

There was always the Rector, living in the rectory beside the church and a succession of clerks who were not rectors (John, Roger, Clement, William and Michael) and also chaplains (Adam, William, Robert, Richard and John) who would be, in turn, the bishops' chaplains serving in the palace chapel. They were frequently mentioned as becoming involved in village affairs and quarrels: this was particularly so in the case of Robert, known as Robert del Brook; he had a sister Emma who married Nicholas Scut, a member of the sheep-farming family.

It may be of interest at this point to consider all the names used by the villagers between 1222 and 1377 and to see the progress of the development of the 'real' surname at Downham. An analysis has been made (Table VIII) of all the names in the extents of 1222 and 1251 and in the court rolls for the years 1310–1327 and 1362–1370. In 1222 about 35% of the villagers had only their Christian names, but by 1251 all but 3.7% had a second name of some sort – a patronymic (Nicholas the son of Simon), a locative name (William of Stoneye), a trade name (Juliana the gardener) or a 'real' surname which was not any of these and which was very often a nickname. By 1310 they all had second names.

The trade name always remained popular whether the holder actually carried on that trade or whether he had inherited the name, but not the trade, from his father. The patronymic was much used in the early periods but by 1310 it was disappearing, giving way to the 'real' surname which was owned by about half the villagers in the two later periods.

The increase in the locative name in the later years shows that many strangers had arrived to settle in the village: by 1370 Downham had received inhabitants from over thirty places – some from other parts of the Isle, others from Cambridgeshire, Norfolk, Suffolk and Bedfordshire and one from as far as Kendal in Westmorland.

Biographies of some of the villagers appear in Chapter XII.

Then there was the lord, the Bishop of Ely. Between the years 1222 and 1377 there were, in succession, twenty-two bishops, listed in Table IX. They were not often in the Downham palace for long periods at a time for, as lords of fifty manors (in six counties), as bishops of a diocese that comprised the county of Cambridge and as great barons owing service to the king, they led peripatetic lives.[1] The bishops were frequently 'beyond the seas', sometimes on church, sometimes on state affairs. Hugh of Northwold was sent by Henry III to

1 Edward Miller, *The Abbey and Bishopric of Ely* (Cambridge, 1969), pp. 77, 75.

Raymund Earl of Provence in 1235 to conclude the marriage contract between the king and the earl's daughter Eleanor, and to conduct the bride to England.[2] Hugh of Balsham was overseas on church affairs in 1262 and in Scotland in 1267, William of Louth went to Jerusalem in 1290, Robert of Orford to Rome in 1302.[3] John of Hotham was sent to the Pope in 1316 to treat concerning the revenues of the Duchy of Aquitaine. In 1318 he was made Chancellor of England.[4] This brought him much travelling away from his diocese, with his household and clerks. In 1323 he was in Gascony 'on the king's service' and also in the following year and in 1326, 1327 and 1330.[5] Nearer home, he was in Yorkshire in 1319, at the English defeat by the Scots at Myton in Swaledale, and afterwards treating for peace with Robert Bruce.[6] In 1328 and again in 1329 he was in Bury St Edmunds 'composing the differences' between that abbey and the townspeople of Bury.[7]

Simon of Montacute's responsibilities involved, in 1330, the collection of certain taxes in the county of Cambridge, including the special tax of 'the ninth' (the ninth lamb, the ninth fleece, the ninth sheaf): in 1341 he was on a commission formed to receive complaints in the county about another tax, the county's share towards the 30,000 sacks of wool granted by Parliament to the king.[8]

Thomas de l'Isle was no such pillar of the establishment. If the complaints about him were true he was utterly irresponsible, in the early years of his episcopacy even threatening a Norfolk farmer (Richard Spynk) and stealing his stock.[9] He was travelling in Europe in 1348 and during the plague years in England he was in Rome.[10] He returned in 1350: the reeve's accounts show journeys by his sister and his brother John to Chatteris and Doddington 'on various occasions' in 1350/51, so he probably spent a good deal of time at Downham that year. In 1354 he had a quarrel with Lady Blanche Wake, a daughter of the Earl of Lancaster, about the boundary between her land at Colne and his at Somersham, in Huntingdonshire.[11] After receiving a court ruling which he considered unjust he complained unwisely to the king. It so happened, shortly afterwards, that one of his men killed one of Lady Blanche's servants and Thomas was convicted of harbouring the killer: afraid of the consequences, he fled to Avignon and remained there until his death in 1361.[12]

---

2 James Bentham, *History and Antiquities of the Conventual and Cathedral Church of Ely* (Cambridge, 1771). p. 146.
3 *Cal. Pat. Rolls*, 1258–66, p. 221; 1266–72, p. 60; 1290, p. 372; 1301–7, p. 45.
4 Bentham, *Cathedral of Ely*, p. 156.
5 *Cal. Pat. Rolls*, 1321–24, pp. 237, 246, 332; 1324–27, pp. 43, 298; 1327–30, pp. 184, 547.
6 Bentham, *Cathedral of Ely*, p. 156.
7 *Cal. Pat. Rolls*, 1327–30, pp. 353, 425.
8 *Cal. Pat. Rolls*, 1338–40, p. 501; 1340–43, p. 315.
9 *Cal. Pat. Rolls*, 1345–48, pp. 186, 188.
10 Bentham, *Cathedral of Ely*, p. 161.
11 *Cal. Pat. Rolls*, 1354–58, p. 162.
12 Bentham, *Cathedral of Ely*, p. 162.

The bishops owned other manor houses in which they stayed besides those at Doddington and Somersham and the palaces at Ely and Downham. There were two more in Cambridgeshire, at Balsham and at Ditton – the latter was rebuilt by Hugh of Northwold and later crenellated by Hugh of Balsham. There were two in Hertfordshire, at Hadham and at Hatfield, and in the Isle there was the castle at Wisbech. And John of Kirkby left in his will 'to the church of Ely' a messuage and nine cottages in Holborn to be held *in mortmain*: this became in time the London mansion of the bishops of Ely.[13]

Three of these bishops concerned themselves with the rebuilding of Ely Cathedral. Hugh of Northwold (1229–1254) completed the West Tower and western transepts, begun before this time, and he rebuilt the choir, demolishing the earlier, Norman, one. His new choir was consecrated in 1252. On 12 February 1322 the central tower collapsed, destroying the three western bays of Northwold's choir. John of Hotham (1316–1337) had appointed Alan of Walsingham as sacrist and the fall of the tower gave Alan his chance: he built the octagon tower and rebuilt the three western bays of the choir, linking the octagon with the eastern bays of Northwold's choir. It was in Simon of Montacute's time (1337–1345) that the octagon was completed and it was he who had the Lady Chapel built.

Hugh of Northwold was also energetic in the repair and rebuilding of the manor houses: he rebuilt a great part of the Ely Palace[14] and also the private room (*camera*) at Downham. He was a man of great vigour and administrative talent – he must be gratefully remembered, too, with John of Fountains, for the extents which throw so much light on the life in the manors at that time.

When the lord was expected at Downham palace there was much ado; the reeves' accounts record work done 'against the lord's coming' – repairing the stables and mangers, cleaning the *camera*, mowing the fen for covering the floors of the *camera* and the hall, mowing rushes (*scirpus*) for making rush-lights, and hunting the fallow deer for the feasting of the lord.

Something can be gleaned from the documents about the more private aspect of the bishop's life. According to the standards of the time the palace must have been a pleasant place to live in: it was surrounded by its great enclosed park and there was also 'the lord's small garden', very private with its new wall, ridged and capped in 1348/49 (D 10/2/18[3]): and there was a pond, but perhaps this was to help with the fish supply. The lord had his private room: a new chimney was built for it in 1320. For the palace fuel, between 40,000 and 80,000 turves were delivered every year, 4,000–12,000 faggots and sometimes coal, up to 27½ cwt. one year. For the floor coverings and repair of roofs 8,000–15,000 bundles of rushes were supplied from the fen. Regular entries are made of some of the food produced on the demesne 'for the lord's larder':

13 Bentham, *Cathedral of Ely*, pp. 163, 151.
14 Bentham, *Cathedral of Ely*, p. 148.

one boar and, on the average, twelve pigs were sent to the hall every year and always the remainder of the fruit from the orchard after about 4s. worth had been sold: this included apples, pears, plums and cherries. The lord had his fisheries in the fen, his deer, rabbits, pheasants and partridges in the park – and when he travelled there went with him a yeoman with a goshawk to ensure the supply of game. And at home he had his dovecot stocked with pigeons – and his vineyard at Ely possibly supplied some of his wine. His household was always large and sometimes enormous but it seems that he must have feasted well.

III. HOLDINGS AND CONDITIONS OF TENURE

The 1251 extent, which differs little from that of 1222, shows the open fields to have comprised 444½ 'acres' of demesne, 294 held by thirty-three customary tenants and (assuming that their lands were in the fields) 158½ acres belonging to four free tenants and 24 held by twenty-four cottars. Vinogradoff[1] suggests that the cotlands may have surrounded the individual dwellings of the holders, but he agrees that the extents certainly suggest otherwise, and that is the assumption held in this study.

Free Tenants

In 1251 the largest holder, Clement, the son of Fulk who had been the tenant in 1222, had a carucate (120 acres). He was a subtenant of the Prior of Ely and owed suit of court and boonwork (harvest work) to the bishop. (The Prior also owed suit of court as tenant.)

The next was Thomas the chaplain, with 28 acres. He had held the same land in 1222. He also owed suit of court and boonwork to the lord and paid rent, three shillings a year.

The Brethren of the Hospital of St John of Ely had 3½ acres (held by Roger le Grand in 1222). The services due were hospitality to the bishop's emissaries and a share of the work in the Ely vineyard and on the Aldreth Causeway. Instead of doing the last duty, they could pay twopence. Although the extent does not mention it, they also owed suit of court: the court rolls record the Master's provision of essoins on two occasions, amercements of sixpence for non-attendance on two more court days and then, four times, payments of a shilling for exemption for one year.

The only free tenant without any services was Giles of Longtown, *de longa villa* (Ralph de Leyton in 1222, perhaps the same name). He held 7 acres for a shilling and sixpence a year. He would certainly owe suit of court[2] though the extent does not say so.

Another freeman, Simon de Ketene, appears in the records on 17 May 1329 when the lord found it wise to have inquiry made on the sale of free lands to villeins and, surprisingly, the sale of customary lands to free men. The inquest found that two freemen had acquired bits of customary land: Simon de Ketene

---

1 Paul Vinogradoff, *Villainage in England* (Oxford, 1968), p. 256.
2 *Ibid.* p. 389.

had bought 2 acres form Richard Kede, a villein, six years previously and the Master of the Hospital had bought 2½ roods from Nicholas Rote.

On the other hand, entries in the roll of 20 May 1327 and 5 December 1328 show that the Prior had sold 10 and 8 acres respectively to Geoffrey Scut and Adam Buk; and the inquests of 17 May 1329 and 19 July 1331 reveal that various freemen had sold to villeins a further 32½ acres (13 to Scut, 10½ to Buk, 9 to various others). These freemen are all unnamed except Thomas Thine, who sold 5½ acres to Adam Buk.

Holders of Full Lands

The full land was the standard holding of 14 nominal acres. In 1251, eleven of the twenty-one full lands were held in partnership by two or three villeins, but throughout the fourteenth century many were divided, instead, into half lands and even quarter lands, all held singly.

The customary duties due from a full land are laid down most minutely in the 1251 survey and the number of works due, the acres to be ploughed and the days to be worked did not vary throughout our period.

These tenants owed three 'works' a week throughout the year and their 'workdays' were Monday, Wednesday and Friday. Their main duty was the ploughing, which they did with their own plough-teams: they had to plough on 'forty Fridays' in the year, ploughing (but not other work) being excused during the eight weeks of harvest (Lammas to Michaelmas), two weeks after Christmas and one week after both Easter and Whitsunday. The ploughing to be done on one day was a sixth of an acre and this counted as one 'work'. Besides this, they had two boon works to perform with the plough: one, 'in Fastnyng-sede', to plough half an acre both in Lent and before Christmas; the other 'in Benerth' (boon-earth: gift ploughing) to plough a rood three times a year, in Lent, in the summer, and after the harvest. For the former they received no pay but for Benerth they received a halfpenny a rood. Every one of them, therefore, was responsible for the ploughing of 6⅔ acres a year for which they received work credits and a further 1¾ acres to be done without credit as boon work. For most boon work food was provided but not for Fastnyng-sede (well-named) or for Benerth.

Harrowing earned one work credit for one day, but here, again, two days, one in winter and one in Lent, had to be done as boon work 'in Benharnynge' (boon harrowing). But on these two days they were given food, a loaf and two herrings, and a saddlebag of oats for their horses.

Hoeing was demanded 'if needed', but for this work a tenant could send his son.

The hay harvest might require his help: a day's mowing was worth one credit. If, besides, he used his own 'cart and horse and ox' to carry the hay to the demesne farm-yard, it was worth two credits. A cheerful note is struck here:

the customary tenants working together in the hayfield and stacking in the farm-yard were given two shillings 'for drinking together'. This would buy about sixteen gallons of ale and how richly they must have deserved it!

In the corn harvest much work was given without credit: in fact, the first day was known as the great boon. The tenant had to present himself in the lord's cornfield with four men, to bind and stook half an acre and carry a load of corn to the demesne farm-yard. For this, two of his men were given food (two loaves, a dish of meat, cheese and beer). On the second day, 'the morrow of the great boon', he had to turn up with three men and reap one acre of corn. For this he had two work credits and two of his men were given food (two loaves, a dish of eels or pollock or six herrings, cheese and water. No beer today!). After that day he must be prepared to come, if needed, to work in the harvest field and carry the corn, with his own cart if necessary, for the appropriate credits. At the end of the harvest he was given a sheaf of corn.

The other duties which he could be called upon to do were:

For one credit
Threshing 24 sheaves of corn (but the first 24 were boon-work).
Winnowing 3 quarters of barley and making malt from it (but the first 3 quarters were boon work).
Cutting 40 bundles of reeds, or 30 bundles and thatching with them.
Digging drainage ditches 5 feet wide and 5 feet deep round the fields (1 perch of new ditch, 2 of old).
Making sheep hurdles from withies.
Splitting and carrying bundles of brushwood for fencing.
Half a day's work on fencing, wood-cutting (for the hall fire or for branches to feed the lord's beasts), dipping and shearing sheep, muck-spreading, etc.

For no credit
Building the garden wall at Ely.
Thatching the Ely bakery.
Digging (with others) 40 perches of the boundary ditch around the park.

There were three duties from which he could be excused on payment of money:

Binding 16 cartloads, of 40 bundles each, of coarse rushes, or pay 4d. 'seggeselver' (sedgesilver).
Working on the Aldreth Causeway for one work, or pay 2d.
Digging in the Ely vineyard for one work, or pay 1d.

Then there were the carrying duties, some by land and some by water from Downham Hythe. There was much carrying to be done when the bishop moved from one to another of his manor houses and many journeys to the place he was occupying at the time. The journeys to Doddington, Chatteris and Manea by boat have been mentioned; they were also made to Somersham by boat and for the journeys to all these places a work credit was given. Much carrying was done to Ely: this was by land and earned no credit unless it was with the lord's luggage. Tenants went to Ely to take the manor's crops to market or wood to the Ely palace, and to fetch salt. They went, for no credit, to other manors for corn and with the bailiff to buy stock at places as far away as Wisbech, St Ives or Bury St Edmunds. But on those long days food was supplied – and in any case they must have been something of an outing.

As well as his duties the customary tenant had dues to pay: 'wytepound' 8d. a year, two hens at Christmas (sometimes capons in the later years), twenty eggs at Easter. He had to pay 'lerewyte' (an unfixed amount, usually 6d.) if his daughter committed adultery and a tax, 'gersuma' on her marriage. At his death, heriot was due, that is, his best beast had to go to the lord, or 32d. if he had no beast: if he held only a half land, this sum was reduced to 16d. (Table X).[3]

Finally, there were restrictions: the tenant owed suit to the court and suit to the mill. He could not sell a colt or an ox which he had raised himself without the lord's permission. The lord's leave had also to be obtained for his daughter's marriage. He could not sell his land without leave, nor could he leave the village.

There was one interesting exception to all this: one customer, Warin the carpenter, who held 12 acres. Instead of doing the half-service and paying the dues which this land carried, he did the woodwork on all the lord's ploughs for six of his 12 acres and for the other six he either paid half a mark or he took charge of the lord's cows, and for this latter duty he was paid 'markingcalf' – the calf of one of the the cows in his charge. Instead of giving hens and eggs and other dues to the lord, he had to give a cheese on Whitsunday, and for one year all his cheese and butter had to go to the lord.

Cottars

For their one-acre lands the 24 cottars had duties mainly similar to those of the other tenants. They had only one work-day, Monday, and had no ploughing or harrowing to do – they would have no plough-teams. A cottar had to send one man to do hoeing one day before and one day after Pentecost, for one work each time. A day's mowing earned him a work: stacking hay in the farm-yard was boon work and for him, alas, there was no ale 'for drinking together'. In the corn harvest, he took one man to 'the great boon' and he and his men were given food. On the second day he had to reap, bind and stook one rood of corn for one work; after that, in the 8½ weeks between Lammas and Michaelmas, he had to reap, bind and stook 9½ acres of corn for nine works 'and when needed he will stack in the barn or farm-yard for a whole day without food or credit for

3 These rates were not fixed until 7 July 1328.

work. But for every whole day he will have a sheaf of corn'. His other duties were the same as those for other tenants except that where they had to thresh 24 sheaves as boon work, he had to thresh only 12; and where they had to bind 16 cartloads of coarse rushes or pay 4d., he had to bind 8 cartloads or pay 2d. Nor did he help with the great ditch around the park.

The dues he had to pay were: 'wytepound' 3d. a year, one hen at Christmas, 10 eggs at Easter. He paid 'lerewyte' and 'gersuma' as the others did, but no heriot was due at his death. His restrictions were the same as theirs, with one added — he had to keep all his sheep in the lord's fold.

Here again, is one interesting exception. One cottar, Jocelyn the Smith, did all the ironwork on the lord's ploughs, supplying the iron and steel and making the plough-shares and coulters. He was therefore excused the payment of hen and eggs and from doing the customary duties, except that he had to pay his 'wytepound' and 'seggeselver', and had to work on the Aldreth Causeway and in the Ely vineyard (or pay 2d. and 1d.) and he had to send a man to the great boon, 'the lord providing food'.

Just as the demesne arable was divided almost equally among the three fields, so it was with the villeins' lands. A nice illustration of this occurred in the leet court of 14 December 1322 when Geoffrey Morris brought a plea of land against Geoffrey Smith, saying that when Robert Morris, his father, had sold to Geoffrey Smith a quarter of a full land, 'to take and receive just as it fell in various strips both from the good land and bad' (*in diversis parcellis tam de bona terra quam de prava*), Geoffrey Smith had taken all his quarter from the better land 'contrary to the custom of the manor'. (Incidentally, this plea failed; Geoffrey Smith disputed the facts, the inquest ruled in his favour and Geoffrey Morris was amerced sixpence for making a false claim.)

Although the tendency to divide and subdivide the full lands increased during the fourteenth century, the original pattern remained and (up to 1375, the latest account examined) the reeve recorded the fixed rents and 'works' due to the lord as due from twenty-one full lands and twenty-four cotlands, even if these lands had been divided or even if some of them were vacant.

Though the pattern remained, however, the actual conditions of tenure underwent various changes when, in the later years, there was the problem of lands left vacant after the Black Death. The first record of the changed conditions (there being a dearth of records for the 1350s) is in the 1361/62 account, where money rents for customary lands are entered from sixteen tenants. The lands thus let, free of duties and services, were eight full lands at 14s. (John Dumfrey's on a four-year lease, the other seven for a year or less), one three-quarter land, three half lands (for six months only) and three and a half cotlands at 3s. a year (one, Simon-atte-Townsend's, for life). In the same account (1361/62) a marginal note tells of 52 acres of 'native [customary] land nil this year' for lack of tenants. The next account (1363/64) shows that only three full lands, and the part-lands, were being let as such for money rents: other vacant holdings (66½ acres of them) were being let piecemeal at a shilling an acre; and this state of things continued to 1375, the acreage let increasing to 87 and then dropping to 75.

It was different with the cotlands: their number increased from three and a half to eleven and they were nearly all on four-year leases. By 1363/64, however, their conditions had changed again: the payment of 3s. a year was no longer a rent but was 'for works', a commutation for services. In fact, from then this tendency again to demand services affected both cotlands and full lands: in 1363 and 1369 two vacant cotlands were let on the old servile terms, for services and dues; similarly in 1366, 1369 and 1376, four half lands and one full land were let in villeinage. In six of these cases the holdings were taken up only after the new tenant had been 'elected by the whole homage' to accept. Two tenants, Robert Wright and William Scut, rebelled against this return to servile tenure. Wright had a full land for which he paid 14s. a year instead of doing services: half of it had belonged to his father who had paid 7s. a year. Scut had a half land which he held for 12s. a year. It was ordered by the court that both men should hold in villeinage: both men were absent and were distrained. At the next court they refused to comply with the order and were this time ordered by the steward to render services and dues. Wright, however, was excused services on one half land for which he continued to pay 7s. a year, so his case at any rate ended in a compromise.

So much for the customary holdings: but there were two other sources of lands available to the tenants, lands free of dues and services: they were the assarted lands and the farmed out portions of the demesne.

It is not known whether parts of the Downham demesne were let to tenants at any time during the thirteenth century: as the surveys do not mention this perhaps it should be assumed that, in these most prosperous days of farming, the lord parted with none of his land. The earliest of the reeve's accounts (for part of 1301/02) also omits any record of rents for demesne lands. By 1318/19, however, 163 of the 441 acres were being farmed out to tenants (Table XI) and after 1321 the tenants' acreage increased to 348, nearly three times that cultivated by the lord. The figure remained high, and so did the rents (Table XII) for about eight years: then, because of the decrease in population (owing to high mortality in 1328) the rents dropped considerably and the tenants' acreage fell to about 250 acres and remained about 250–270 until 1352. After that date there was land to spare in abundance: the place was so depopulated that, owing to shortage of labour, the demesne could not be tilled and, owing to the shortage of tenants, much of the demesne could not be let. It was indeed taken back into the demesne but not for sowing. The rent account for 1361/62 has a footnote: '341 acres of demesne land nil this year' because tenants could not be found, and from 1361 to 1375 only about 250 acres of the demesne were being cultivated.

There are no records of the names of tenants who farmed demesne lands, except for isolated entries in the court rolls and in the reeve's accounts, and except for two lists: one, the rent roll for 1369/70 giving 78 names, the other, an entry in the court roll for 1 December 1373 giving 23 names. Both these lists give not only the names of the tenants and the amounts of rent, but also the names of the fields or *culturae* in which the lands lay (Appendices I and II).

Assarted lands are not mentioned in the 1222 survey and it seems that at that time the population had not increased to such an extent that extra land, beyond the fields and the meadows, had become a necessity. By 1251, however, we hear of two lots of such land — the old assarts, 69 acres at Apesholt (perhaps where Apeshall now is) let at a penny an acre to fourteen customary tenants and cottagers; and the new assarts, 12½ acres, let at eightpence a year to six tenants and cottagers, four of whom had land also at Apesholt. It is seen that the new assarts commanded the same rent as, later, did much of the demesne arable land and one can only assume that the old assarts had been allowed to deteriorate. Perhaps all the assarted lands met with the same fate by about 1330 when, with the low rents, it must have been preferable for the tenants to transfer their attentions to the demesne lands.

The 1251 extent also lists eight tofts, described as messuages. The Oxford Dictionary defines a messuage as 'a dwelling-house with its outbuildings and curtilage and the adjacent land assigned to its use' and it defines the word 'toft' as used in 1290 as 'the site of a house and its outbuildings'. It seems clear, therefore, that the tofters all had a bit of land. One toft was let at a shilling a year, four at sixpence and the rest at fourpence. Only one of the tenants can be identified from the lists of customary tenants and cottagers and that is Ivo the Red, but whoever they were they all had to do boon-work at harvest, 'the lord providing food'.

IV. THE FEN

To get some idea of the mediaeval fen that stretched beyond the fields of Downham it is well to pay a visit to Wicken Sedge Fen, still preserved in its natural state. There grow the willows and alders and, most prolifically, the purging buckthorn, *Rhamnus catharticus*, the kind of woodland that must have supplied material for building and fuel for the men of Downham and for which they were granted the rights of 'hous-bôte' and 'fir-bôte'. At Wicken, underfoot, is the peat (the *turba* of the Court Rolls) and the tussocky grass like that on which the Downham men grazed their stock. And there, in great profusion, over the length and breadth of the fen, grows the giant reed, *Phragmites communis*. This is the *tegumen* of the extent and the *arundis* of the bailiff's accounts. And there is the sedge, *Cladium mariscus* (the *grossi rosci* of the extent and the *lesch* of the Court Rolls) bending its long leaves over and giving those areas of the fen their strangely shaggy appearance. The spiked edges of these leaves can tear the flesh if not handled with care and the customary duty of sedge-cutting cannot have been a pleasant one.

The fen was no mere playground to the villagers: to some of them it was a way of life, and it was a tremendous asset to them all. As well as the fishing and the fowling in the pools and waterways there was the grazing and mowing in the drier parts: this has already been mentioned. They had to common in 'part of West Fen and of East Fen and North Fen from Westhey to Wellenhey and from Wellenhey to Berecwerehale . . . in Langwood Fen from Westhey to Eathertilond . . . in Baltasmore from Foxlode through Huniholte to the Wimblington meadow' and 'in Welpingmorbrendefen' and 'on the great bank of Church Fen but it must not be mown'. It would be interesting to trace these limits of the common fen but the only easily recognizable place-names are Welney, five miles north, Wimblington, seven miles north-west, and Langwood Fen five miles west of Downham. At any rate, the grazing land was extensive.

The 'tussocks' referred to earlier as 'growing over six acres of fen which could be cleared', were of tussock sedge, *Carex paniculata*, which can grow to four feet high and three feet wide. It would certainly be necessary to cut the tussocks back before meadowing could be considered.

Then there was the peat.[1] The peat was, of course, valuable fuel. The villeins, for another customary duty, had to dig it and make turves for the lord:

1 A fascinating account of the formation of peat fen and its ecology is given in Harry Godwin's *'Fenland: Its Ancient Past and Its Uncertain Future'* (Cambridge 1978).

on 30 November 1375 four of them were presented for neglecting this. They could also dig it for their own use and for sale within the vill, but not for sale outside. For the offence of selling outside the vill the normal amercement was only threepence a thousand throughout these years and the presentments were numerous: the rolls record 242. The value of the turves is quoted only once, on 16 December 1325, when they were worth a shilling for 500, so it was well worth while to ply this trade.

The sedge, *Cladium mariscus*, was used for thatching the cottages and for the ridging of the better thatches for which reeds were used. It would also be used, probably, in building the cottage walls in the wattle and daub method. Reference has been made to the mowing and binding of sedge as a customary duty and, as in the case of turves, those who had the right of common, 'commoners', were allowed to cut it for their own use or for sale within the vill. They were forbidden to sell it beyond the 'boundary of Downham' (Court Rolls 18 June 1315) and, so that it might be allowed to grow, they were forbidden to cut it between Michaelmas and Hokeday (the Tuesday after Low Sunday).

The Court Rolls show 185 instances of villeins' being presented for selling sedge outside the vill. The normal amercement was 6d. for a thousand. The value of the sedges is never mentioned but the sale must have been profitable or it would surely not have persisted. There were other presentments concerning sedge: two for cutting before Hokeday; seventeen on one day in 1315 for cutting 'not being commoners' (and one of these carted his sedges to Ely). Another offence was to leave the sedge unbound on the fen after cutting it.

Withies were another product of the fen and were used for hurdles, the making of which was another customary duty and another bonus for any tenant who had his own sheepfold.

To maintain discipline in fenland matters, special custodians were appointed or elected in court. Thus, on 29 April 1326 and again on 27 June 1373, three jurors were given the responsibility of keeping the fen in 'safety and security'. Their duties included, besides the protection from fire of the highly inflammable growth in summer, the presenting of any who took from the fen more wood than was allowed by 'hous-bôte' or 'fir-bôte', the presenting of any non-commoners who grazed stock on Downham lands and the impounding of this stock. In court on 13 March 1376 they were at work, presenting six cases of selling turves and one of selling 'lesch', outside the vill, and presenting two men, Simon, son of John Cok, and John, son of Richard Wright, who 'on Monday in the Feast of St. Matthew . . . set fire to and burned the fen called Whyte-fen, behind Les Hundred Acres of land so that the whole of the said fen was burned'. This was so serious an offence that an order was made 'to seek the advice of the lord's council'; this is the only occasion through these years on which such advice was sought. At the next court, on 5 July 1376, the two appeared again with a third man, John Lovechild, and they were all amerced forty pence.

There was an earlier case of fen-burning, on 11 May 1334, when two men (or boys), William le Hirde and Simon, the boy of Richard Aleyn, 'lit a fire in the fen, contrary to the rules, and burned the Westmoor to the annoyance of the whole vill'. An order was made to attach them and produce them at the next court 'to answer to the lord'. One of them, William, did not turn up in court on 31 August 1334 'to answer the lord bishop in a plea as to why they burned the Westmoor' and in consequence his four pledges were all amerced at 12d. Unfortunately this is the one case on that day for which the amount of the amercement of an offender is not entered, but judging from the amount not accounted for in the total, it can be assumed that the boys were charged 3s. 4d. each, as in the later cases. This may well have been six weeks' pay.

V. THE BYLAW AND OFFICERS OF THE VILL

1. The Bylaw

In the Downham court, on 1 July 1311, the jurors presented ten Downham men for cutting 'fodder on the common land before the Feast of St John the Baptist [24 June] which was against the ruling about the seasons, etc.' And in that same court the 'entire homage' (probably just the chief pledges) elected nine of their number 'to see to the keeping of the rules made in court concerning crops and the preserving of the meadowlands of the lord and others, and concerning the fen and the turves, and to present at the following court any transgressors against these rules'. This is the earliest reference, in these papers, to a body of men later referred to as the custodians of the bylaw, and the Court Roll shows that by 31 July 1314 the number had been increased to ten, and so it remained to 24 September 1325. The following year, on 29 April 1326, two of these ten, and one other man, were elected as custodians of the fen and it seems that the specialised care of the fen was transferred to them from the custodians of the bylaw, for by 1 August 1334 the latter had reduced their number to six. From then their concern would not be with the fen at all, but almost entirely 'concerning the crops and the preserving of the meadowlands of the lord and others'.

The Downham bylaw, which, like that of other vills, must have been made and amended by the court to suit the village's particular needs, is not quoted in these papers. Some idea of its scope, however, can be gathered from the cases presented in court as 'contrary to the bylaw' and these covered various sins.

The rule broken most frequently was the one forbidding damage to another's crops. About fifty such cases are recorded: the damage was nearly always caused by animals. In December 1324 the reeve (in charge of the lord's calves) and the lord's swineherd had allowed their charges to stray into Katharine the hayward's wheat: the rector had done likewise with his pigs and five others with their oxen. The amercements totalled a shilling and eightpence, but damages of three shillings were awarded and an order was made for this sum to be levied and paid to Katharine. In September 1331 John Hayt had depastured a horse in the cabbages 'contrary to the bylaw': three others had done likewise, and seven had had pigs in the corn.

There were rules concerning the grazing in the stubble; on the one hand, the fields should not be entered by animals before the crops were carried and on the other hand, the carrying of crops should not be unnecessarily delayed and the animals thus excluded. Thus, in October 1324 the wardens of the bylaw presented that Geoffrey Smith 'did not carry the lord's corn at the proper time', and 'all of the homage who had horses broke the bylaw by keeping their horses in the fields by night before crops were carried, contrary to the said regulation'. There may have been a special rule concerning horses, forbidding their presence, tethered or not, in a field where there was grain; such a rule existed in other places.[1] There were bylaw offences connected with gleaning: twenty are recorded for gleaning badly and it was ordered that if a person was able to reap, then he or she must do so, and not glean. On 25 September 1327 the wardens presented six cases of women who had 'done no reaping but had gleaned'; on 10 September 1331 they presented Thomas atte hythe and three women for gleaning badly. One of these women, Amicia, the daughter of John Child, broke another rule of the bylaw: she 'took some corn'. This taking of sheaves of corn from the harvest field was a great temptation. In 1324, on 15 October, fourteen such presentments were made and on 19 December 'Richard Kede received from Gareth the warrener half a bushel of corn stolen in the harvest, contrary to the bylaw'. Various ways were devised to prevent this theft: one was to regulate the number of sheaves to constitute a cartload, for it would be an easy matter to shed a couple of sheaves on the way to the farm-yard where they would not be missed from an allegedly full load. On 25 September 1327, Clement the brewer was presented for breaking this rule: he had 'carted two sheaves over and above his cartload'.

Perhaps another precaution against the theft of sheaves was the rule against reaping with people from outside the vill. Three men were presented for this on 31 August 1334: they had 'reaped the lord's corn with strangers, by choice and not with their own servants'.

2. The Officers

The reeve and the hayward were the leading figures in this disciplined and organized community. They were always customary tenants, holders of full lands. They had no wages but because of their duties their 'works' were excused, as were the customary annual payments of hens and eggs to the lord. During the four or five weeks of harvest they fed 'at the lord's table', the accounts showing this expense at 1½d. a day for each of the men in the earlier years, and later usually 1d. a day but it was then supplemented by a bushel of wheat at 8d. a bushel for each of them at the end of the harvest.

Perusal of the reeve's accounts, already described in the Introduction, reveals how wide was his authority. The recto shows that he was responsible for all monies received: the 'fixed rents' of the tenants (the 'wytepund' and 'segge-selver' referred to in the extent of 1251), the rents for farm of lands, fisheries

1. W.O. Ault, *Open Field Farming in Medieval England* (London, 1972).

and mill, the profits from sales of grain, stock and 'works', and the perquisites of the court. This income was to cover his expenditure in all the farming departments and also in the building work done on the demesne, including repairs to the lord's palace. He rendered his account annually, presumably dictating it to a scribe (from memory and reference to tallies), and he was held answerable for any deficit, this being entered as 'arrears, owing to the lord'.

He had to deal with many problems in the later years when the village was badly depopulated and there was much real poverty.[2] The court directed that the reeve should be held answerable for all the vacant holdings – and in 1362 and the following years these were equivalent to seven full lands and six cotlands. He no doubt concerned himself also with the neglected and dilapidated holdings and cottages whose occupants had been ordered to do repairs, for failure to carry out the court's order led to confiscation of the holding and its being entrusted to the reeve. He was ordered by the court to trace fugitives from the manor, and if they were captured he was in charge of them until the next court. It seems that they usually managed to evade capture. The stray animals brought another duty to the reeve: they appeared from other villages across the common grazing lands and the court ordered that he should be in charge of them until they were claimed by their owners. Sometimes the period of detention was considerable: at the end of June 1369 the reeve was given charge of a bull, two heifers and five mares. The heifers and two mares were claimed in September and two more mares the following May, but the bull and one mare remained in his care until the end of July 1370 when, the roll records, having been kept for 'a year and a day', they became the property of the lord.

The reeve was, in fact, the agent of the court and thus carried great responsibility in the administration of the vill as well as in the management of the demesne. He needed to be a man of many parts. Surprisingly he only twice made presentments (in September 1330 and in May 1364) and this suggests that, being involved with the wider administration of the demesne and vill, he left disciplinary details to the hayward. In very many courts, however, he is recorded as standing pledge for villagers.

In the record of the court proceedings of 27 February 1316 the reeve, William Personn, was himself presented by the jurors for having committed fifteen offences. These included the use of one of the lord's servants for stacking his own corn and the use of the lord's horses and oxen on various occasions for carting his own timber, sedges, turves and peas (and overtired one horse: 'indeed the horse was old, nevertheless they say that at that time it was worth three shillings'): he had neglected properly to supervise carters bringing stone for building part of the palace and they had stolen oats and fodder from the barn: he had overcharged for grain used for the lord's horses and had extracted too large a fine from a swineherd who, through neglect, had caused the death of

2 See Chapter VIII: Administration of village affairs.

three of the lord's pigs. One unproved charge concerned his control of plough teams. Personn was amerced 10s. and charged damages amounting to 25s. 10d. and was dismissed 'by the whole homage' who elected Simon Cardinal to succeed him as *prepositus manerii*. This is the only instance in these papers in which this office is so described: at all other times, in the court rolls and at the head of the accounts, it is entered as *prepositus*.

There were also minor officers who appear in the later court rolls as *prepositi*. They were elected, two at a time, by the September courts in 1364, 1370, 1374 and 1376, Nicholas the son of Simon being elected three times, William Hayt three times and John Lovechild twice. (Nicholas seems to have coupled this work with that of hayward for he resigned from both offices at Michaelmas 1367.) There are no accounts for the years beginning at Michaelmas 1364, 1370 and 1376 but that for 1374/75 shows that John Wrong, whose name is in the heading, was certainly the reeve of the manor in that year so these others must have held some lesser office such as reep-reeve. A reep-reeve is mentioned once, in the early years: in September 1312 he presented, with the reeve, an offender who had cut the grass on the baulks between the lord's strips of barley.

About the election or appointment of the reeves of the manor and the periods of their service: the earliest instance of an election is the one referred to above, that of Simon Cardinal in 1316 after the dismissal of William Personn. Apart from this isolated case there is no mention in the earlier series of rolls (to 1334/45) of the election or resignation of any reeve. In the later series, it is shown that on 16 March 1362 John Wrong was elected in court: he first appears at the head of the reeve's accounts for the year 1361/62 (Table III) and he is shown thus as reeve on all the five existing accounts thereafter, including the last, that for 1374/75. It seems reasonable, although some accounts are missing, to assume that he was reeve of the manor from Michaelmas 1361 to (at any rate) Michaelmas 1375. Table III shows another reeve of the manor, Geoffrey Cardinal, to have held office, possibly, for the fifteen years from 1331/32 to 1346/47 (certainly from 1341/42 to 1346/47) and then, after a year's gap, to Michaelmas 1352. The rest served for six or four years or less.

There was not, in Downham, any non-law-abiding hayward with a helpful record of offences to pin-point his duties. On one occasion, however, on 28 January 1326, the court roll tells of a special election of a second, or assistant, hayward, John le Eyr who 'in a meeting and by the assent of the whole 'county' and vill of Downham, had been elected hayward for the care of the corn growing the the fields, etc.' This underlines the hayward's main duty, for the community and for the lord, of containing the stock from doing damage. His frequent presentments in court mainly dealt with this matter: on 18 court days he presented a total of 59 offenders for damaging the lord's crops or meadows and 14 offenders for other transgressions (refusing to do 'works', bad work in the harvest field and one for breaking pound – extracting an impounded animal). He did not, however, present all the cases of damage to the lord's crops and meadows: the jurors did this work on 34 other court days, presenting a further 165 of these offenders.

On most of the court days the hayward stood pledge for one tenant or another, sometimes for several, mostly in cases of entry into land and requests for leave to agree, but very often also for one or other of the parties to a complaint of debt or damage. Occasionally he was the pledge of a defendant in some criminal case such as assault or slander.

There is little evidence of it, but it seems that he may have been involved in normal collection of monies (fines and amercements) for the court, for in May 1374 he was ordered to collect the 60s. recognisance money which was always payable to a new lord. Perhaps, therefore, all court collections were his responsibility.

Haywards were elected in court, but it was not always recorded in the roll that an election or resignation had taken place: there are more gaps in the series than those caused by missing membranes. The earlier rolls, however, give the dates of both election and resignation of four haywards. One served from September 1325 to December 1328, the next for one year from December 1328: he then paid 6d. for the privilege of resigning. The next served for one year from December 1329 and another for one year from September 1333. In the later series of rolls there are five recorded elections of haywards, two at a time, in 1362, 1364, 1370, 1374 and 1376, but no resignations are entered.

The custodians of the byelaw and the custodians of the fen have already been mentioned. Besides these there were special custodians of certain waters, the dyke-reeves appointed in connection with the commission for sewers (drains).[3] Six jurors were appointed on 5 December 1328 as dyke-reeves of the New Ditch 'which the lord had drained. No one is to fish in it or place a fish-trap or nets [in it] ... or to cross it with planks or in any other way. And if anyone finds transgressors he is ordered to give evidence in court concerning the offences'. Three dyke-reeves (all jurors) were appointed on 5 July 1376 as supervisors of the lode from Downham Hythe to Manea.

The matter of enclosure was watched: twelve jurors, the custodians of the vill, were appointed on 7 July 1328 'to present all enclosures'. Presumably some temporary enclosure of assarted land was in order: enclosure in the fields would always be illicit.

Then there was the constable, elected by the homage; there was the election of John de Columbers on 13 December 1329. Incidentally, on the same

---

3 Various commissions of sewers were issued by the King from the mid-thirteenth century onwards. The duties of the commissioners were to organize the drainage work already being done locally 'by ancient custom', to find out what further work was required, to supervise all work and (where necessary) compel those responsible to get it done. [H.C. Darby, '*The Mediaeval Fenland*' (Newton Abbot, 1974), pp. 155–6; and H.C. Darby, '*The Draining of the Fens*' (Cambridge, 1968), p. 1.]

day he had been attached to answer a complaint of debt of 13s. due the previous Michaelmas, but this would hardly affect the duties he would have to perform. As now, the constable's lot was not always a happy one though none of his troubles appear until the later years when, on 3 December 1364, John Taillour was presented for obstructing the constable Richard Snow, in contempt of the lord king and he 'did not wish to justify himself'.

Perhaps the constables of the watch should be mentioned here, though they were not regular officers of the vill. Because of the general lawlessness at the time it was laid down in the Statute of Winchester (1285) that in every borough, town, or vill a number of men, four or more according to the size of the place, must keep watch at night from sunset to sunrise. The men of Downham would take turns to do this duty, four at a time. The court record of 1 December 1373 tells of assault on the four: Simon Hert was attacked by John, son of Cecilia Holt and Stephen Frost set upon the other three, Geoffrey Cardinal, William son of Simon atte Townesend and Adam Kede 'with weapons, preventing them from doing the service of the lord king'.

Other officers mentioned in these papers are those to do with the quality of the animals of the vill. On 29 April 1326 two jurors were appointed as coroners of stock to superintend the buying and selling of stock and to present any defect in them; and in the sad later years when many animals were dying of the 'murrain' inspectors of carcases were appointed in court, to determine the cause of death. This precaution seems to have been mainly on the lord's behalf: no action is ever recorded to have been taken because of death by murrain, but if the death was caused through the neglect of the keeper of the animal, steps were taken to prevent this occurring again.

Another office, also concerning the stock, was perhaps rather an employment than an office. It was that of the common herdsman who undertook the custody of the villeins' beasts. One John Hayt did this work in 1332, for 'various men from Downham Hythe for looking after their cows in summer' for which they owed him, but did not pay him, the sum of 4s. The lord gave him help to raise this money, for which help he paid the lord 3d. (February 1333). Another herdsman, years later, had difficulty in getting his wages. On 4 March 1370 William Chephird complained in court that Hugo Prest owed him 10d., 'his pay for the custody of his beasts'. This may have been a private employment, or the 10d. may have been Hugo's share of the pay of the common herdsman. The office of 'attendant of stock' appears in the record of 13 March 1376 when two jurors were elected for this purpose. Their duties are not defined: perhaps they appointed the herdsman and saw that he got paid – one can only guess.

Then, lastly, there were the ale-tasters. Ale and bread, both rich in protein, were important parts of the mediaeval diet and it was important that when sold they should be up to standard in quality and quantity. The assize of bread and ale was held at every leet court, usually in December, and presentments were made for 'breaking the assize', making or selling bread or ale that was substandard or insufficient in quantity (Tables IV – VII). These papers do not reveal who was responsible for checking the bread, but checked it was and occasionally found wanting – but not very often: there were only twenty presentments for poor baking or for selling light-weight loaves against 258 presentments of brewsters or alewives for their various offences. If was the duty of every brewster as soon as fresh ale had been brewed, to send for the ale-taster to test it: to fail to do this was an offence and so was the failure to correct any deficiency that he pointed out. It was the duty also of one selling ale to a customer to measure it first in a leather jug marked, as the imperial pint of today is marked, to show the appropriate measure. There were quart measures, two-quart measures known as pottles and gallon measures. These had to be taken to every leet to be inspected or, if new, to be stamped. One common offence was that of failing to have the measure stamped, another was that of failing to produce it at the leet. Thirty-one of these offences are recorded. All this took care of the quantity of the ale; it was the job of the ale-tasters to check the quality.

Ale was brewed in many of the houses in the vill: there were certainly ten brewsters in 1310 for ten were in the court of 24 November 1310, with five alewives (the alewives sold, but did not brew, the ale). Up to 1335 there were normally three ale-tasters; from 1362 (after the 26-year gap in the court roll) there were only two. They were elected in court by the homage and kept office for various periods, generally from one to five years; there was no fixed pattern. It seems remarkable that on twenty-five occasions the ale-tasters were before the leet for 'failing to fulfill their duty' for it would seem to have been a pleasant enough duty. In what way they failed is never indicated. Perhaps it was inconvenient to go and taste the ale when asked. Perhaps they did taste it and, for fear of the brewster, did not condemn the ale if it was bad. Perhaps the amercements of the ale-tasters were a sort of regular tax, like the 'common fine' paid by the chief pledges at the leet. This may well be the explanation, too, of the regular amercements of some of the brewers and alewives; they could have been a kind of licence fee not bound too rigidly by the assize.

VI. THE COURT: (1) GENERAL

Location

The court was held at Downham and, as one would expect, it was held at the palace. We have nice evidence of this in the reeve's accounts (D 10/2/27) which record the delivery of 2000 turves to the palace especially for the court hearings of the year 1374/75. This was one of the vacancy years between the bishoprics of John Barnet, who died in 1373, and Thomas of Arundel who came in April 1376. So, the palace being without a resident, the turves normally made and sent to the lord as a customary duty would not be delivered.

Dates

The dates of the court were variable. The court year ended at Michaelmas when the perquisites for the year were reckoned for the reeve's annual account. The bishop exercised his right to hold the leet with the view of frankpledge and, throughout, this great court was held annually in November or December (once, in 1365, in October), the manorial courts occurring one on the day of the leet and others at varying intervals during the rest of the year. Up to 1335 (after which year there is a 26-year gap in the court membranes) the intention seemed to be to hold four, or later five, manorial courts a year: once there were only three and once there were six. After the 'gap years' there was a tendency towards more frequent law days: in the twelve of those years for which records remain, one year had seven courts and three had eight: the rest had four or five (Tables I and II).

Suitors

The free tenants and the customary tenants of Downham all owed suit of court. At the time of the 1251 extent there were four free tenants of whom two, the prior of Ely and the Brethren of the Hospital of St John of Ely, were holders *in mortmain.* The prior of Ely was a suitor throughout the period, the successive priors defaulting, proffering essoins 'of the common suit' and paying fines to be excused from court attendance for one year. The Brethren of the Hospital are replaced by the Master of the Hospital by 1311, an entry in the court roll of 9 November 1311 showing that the Master who had defaulted 'owed suit for the holding acquired by fee of tenure from the lord before Christmas'. Successive

30

masters, like the priors, appear throughout as reluctant attenders at court.

There is no record of default by villeins, except when they were required for a plea, until May 1334, when three were charged with that offence. It seems reasonable to suppose that there was some non-attendance but it was disregarded. After the gap in the court rolls (1336–1361), however, cases of absence occurred frequently, some in nearly every court. The amercements varied between 2d. and 6d.

Procedure

The scope of the leet and that of the *curia* are described in detail below, but first the procedure by which these courts performed their various functions must be examined.

Criminal cases, whether in leet or *curia*, had to be brought to the notice of the court by the process of presentment. The procedure of presentment by the jury arose out of the ancient duty of the capital pledges to report the misdoings of the men in their respective tithings. This procedure was originally used only in the leet and higher courts, not in the manorial courts; but by the fourteenth century it was being used indiscriminately in Downham, both in the leet for lesser pleas of the crown and in the manorial court for minor offences against the lord, the court and the community. Serious offences, such as assault, against another tenant were also presented by the jurors but otherwise a tenant had normally to bring his own complaint to get redress and damages by civil action.

Frequently the rolls do not show by whom the cases were presented – the record merely states that 'it was presented that . . .' Clearly, however, presentments were mostly made by the twelve jurors. The hayward is shown to have introduced about one-third of the cases that concerned his special responsibilities. The custodians of the bylaw are recorded in this capacity only seven times and the custodians of the fen only twice, in January 1369 when they dealt with the cutting of 'lesch' after the appointed day and in March 1376 when the fen had been burned. On the latter occasion they also presented seven offenders for selling turves and 'lesch' beyond the vill, a matter which certainly concerned them, but on all the many other occasions this offence was presented by the jurors – as was, also, another case, in November 1375, of cutting 'lesch' after the appointed day.

As the jurors or others presented offences of which they knew the circumstances, it was considered that further evidence was unnecessary. The very act of presentment of a villein found him guilty and he was at once amerced – put in the mercy of the court, *in misericordia*. The jury of presentment was thus also the jury of judgment, judging on behalf of the whole homage. Rarely, very rarely, was the outcome of a presented case disputed and referred to the other jury, the jury of inquest.

The civil cases were brought by the injured parties. Both plaintiff and defendant had to appear: the defendant was summoned and if he failed to appear was allowed essoins at the next three courts before being attached and then distrained of property. Evidence was given on both sides and any cases of dispute (and there were very many) were referred to the jury of inquest who decided the matter and considered, also, the amount of the damages. Often all this took place on the same day and all that is learned from the roll is the result of the inquest. Sometimes, however, the case was heard, and the application for an inquest made, on one law day and the decision given on the next, as on 30 January 1331 when 'the hayward was ordered to bring twelve men to the next court' for the purpose. This is the only reference in these papers to the number of men required for an inquest or to the manner in which one was assembled. An alternative to an inquest was the custom, little used, of 'waging law', which involved bringing a number of witnesses to the next court: waging law 'four-handed' required four witnesses and so on.

If the defendant in a civil case was found to be in the wrong, he paid an amercement as well as damages: if the plaintiff was found to be at fault he was amerced for making a false claim or complaint.

Something must be said about pledges. A pledge stood for a complainant or a defendant in a civil case, or for a defendant in a presented case, to vouch for his attendance, his good faith and his ability to pay any money required of him by the court. This system of pledging was followed in the Downham court during the whole of the period covered by the earlier series of the rolls. It was not, however, followed with consistency: a certain type of case might carry pledges on one law day but not on the next. The matter is worth examination, not only to discover any pattern that may have existed, but also to find the extent of the responsibility of the reeve and, especially, the hayward here.

First of all, to dispose of those cases that did not require a pledge: these included all cases under the bylaw (which embraced the numerous complaints of damage to another tenant's crops and also the sales of turves and 'lesch' outside the vill) and all cases under the assize of bread and ale and under the view of frankpledge. There were very few exceptions to this rule.

Pledges are recorded, but by no means always, in manorial cases such as entry into land, requests for leave to agree, leave to marry or leave to have an inquest, in cases of debt or damages, and in presented cases excluding those mentioned above as requiring no pledge. Much of the pledging was done by the reeve and hayward. Examination of the matters that most attracted pledges shows that:

(1) In the seven years from 1301 to 1316:

a. In 26 cases of entry into land, 16 pledges are recorded, the reeve standing on 2 occasions, the hayward 11.

b. In 28 requests for leave to agree, 25 pledges, the reeve 5, the hayward 7.

32

c. In 18 cases of debt, 13 pledges, the reeve one, the hayward 5.

d. In 10 cases of assault, 10 pledges, the reeve 3, the hayward 3.

(2) In the four years from 1322 to 1325:

a. In 24 entry cases, 8 pledges, the reeve 2, the hayward 4.

b. There were no requests for leave to agree.

c. In 7 cases of debt only one was pledged and it was not by the reeve or the hayward.

d. In 4 assault cases, 4 pledges, the reeve none, the hayward 2.

(3) In the ten years from 1326 to 1335:

a. In 50 entry cases, 37 pledges, the reeve 6, the hayward 9 and (unusually) the steward stood pledge once.

b. In 29 requests for leave to agree, 23 pledges, the reeve none, the hayward 8.

c. In 55 cases of debt only 23 pledges, the reeve one, the hayward 8.

d. In 13 assault cases, 9 pledges, the reeve one, the hayward 2 and the constable stood pledge once.

It will be seen that up to 1335 pledging remained usual for cases of entry and requests for leave to agree, but that by that time it had become much less frequent in cases of debt and of assault. It seems that by then the custom was beginning gradually to die out. Later, by 1362, it had virtually disappeared and pledges were rarely in evidence except when a villager was before the court for allowing his tenement to fall into disrepair (and the pledge was made for the rebuilding) or when a suitor in a plea had failed to appear in court. Apart from these two matters there are only 32 references to a pledge in the last 63 courts between 1362 and 1376, 10 for entry into land, 6 for assault and the rest for various matters

The pledges standing for those whose tenements were in disrepair appear in 13 courts between 1362 and 1376. The hayward was not among them but the reeve stood pledge on three of these occasions, always with another villager. The pledges standing for non-attending suitors appear in 21 of these courts, the reeve standing on 4 occasions (once with the bailiff, once with the hayward and twice with other villagers) and the hayward standing on 8 occasions (once with the reeve and at other times with other villagers). The burden and, often, the expense of pledging was therefore shared, which was fortunate, for on 19 of the 21 occasions when suitors had failed to appear, the pledges were amerced. The amercement was not high, it was usually 2d., but it did come their way fairly often.

Amercements and Fines

No punishment is recorded in these papers except that of amercement which occurred in nearly every case. The most frequent rates of amercements were 3d. and 2d.: these were, respectively, a day's wage of a skilled and an unskilled man. Every now and then a defendant is excused 'because he is poor'.

For 'breaking the assize' the erring brewster, alewife or 'regrater of bread' was nearly always amerced 3d., but sometimes 6d., 8d. or even a shilling as in a case of the sale of sub-standard bread. Tithing offences were never more than 3d.: default was 3d. or, for the regulars, 6d.

Amercements for assault generally matched the offence: 2d., 3d. or 4d. for beating, 6d., 9d. or 12d. for 'drawing blood'. For theft amercements varied from 6d. to (in the case of stealing corn) 2s. Defamation of character was never more than 2d. or 3d. but slander on one occasion cost 2s. Debt was usually 2d. or 3d., occasionally 6d.: false complaints always 2d. or 3d.

Offences against the lord were amerced no more highly than others: damage to his crops or park was usually 3d. though sometimes 6d. or 8d. On one occasion when the park was invaded by piglets the cost to their owners varied in proportion to their numbers, from 4d. for 2 piglets to 4s. for 24. Keeping sheep 'not in the lord's fold' could cost as little as 3d. but more often the amercement was more or less in line with the number of sheep involved: 15 sheep and lambs costing 12d., 40 or 50 sheep costing 18d. Refusal to work cost the culprit surprisingly little, only 2d. or 4d. (once it was 6d.). To marry without leave was amerced in accordance with the fine that would have been charged if the 'request for leave to marry' had been properly made, usually 1s. or 2s.

Offences that affected the whole community (bylaw offences and some others) also earned a variety of amercements. Damages to other tenants' crops always cost 2d., 3d. or 4d., bad gleaning 6d., encroachment on the common, or on the road, or obstruction to any drain, would be amerced at 2d., 3d. or occasionally 6d. Failure to help with the work on the causeway earned a high amercement, 12d. So, also, did the failure to join a plough team which was a serious matter, as was the cutting of fodder before St John the Baptist's Day, 24 June, which cost 6d., 1s. or even 2s. For selling turves and 'lesch' outside the vill the amercements (6d. for 1000 'lesch' and 3d. for 1000 turves) remained unchanged throughout the whole period of these papers – except on two unfortunate occasions (16 December 1325 and 4 December 1326) when an angry steward was faced with an exceptionally high number of transgressors who had been selling both commodities. On the first day there were twenty amercements at 2s. a thousand for 'lesch', and twelve amercements at 10d. a thousand for turves. The next time there were fifteen amercements and the rates dropped to 1s. and 10d. respectively and after that they returned to normal.

For all these transgressions the rates were fairly stable throughout, except on a few occasions when possibly the affeerers were influenced by the steward. The charges were not greater at the end of the period than at the beginning.

Certain fines were charged in court and these, like the amercements, did not increase as time went on, but some varied considerably. The fine for 'leave to agree' was always 3d. or 2d; that for leave to marry varied a good deal, perhaps with the circumstances of the people concerned; for a villein to marry a villein's daughter usually cost 1s. or 2s. but on one occasion it was 6d. and sometimes it was 3s. 4d. To make a request for an inquest might cost 3d., 6d. or 12d. and whether it was to be an inquest over a boundary or over a disputed complaint or other matter did not seem to influence the rate. The 'gersuma' rates, the fines paid on entry into land, are dealt with in Chapter VIII, with the rates of 'heriot' and other matters concerning land transfer.

The Jurors (Tables XIII and XIV)

In the earlier years, up to 1335, the jurors are listed in leet records only. There are 17 leet records for this period but only 14 of them contain jury lists and these lists are headed 'Jurors'. In the later years, from 1362, the jurors are listed in both leet and manorial court records: there are 62 of these (10 leet and 52 manorial), but only 49 of them (8 leet and 41 manorial) contain lists. The lists for the leet are headed 'Capital Pledges' or 'Capital Pledges or Jurors' and those for the manorial court are headed 'Jurors ex officio'.

From the fact that they were identifed with the capital pledges, one assumes the jurors to have been men of good standing in the vill and the matter of their status seems to be worth investigation. There are no lists of customary tenants and cotlanders later than those of the 1251 extent, but from the records of land transfers in the court rolls and from the entries of heriot payments in the reeves' accounts, the status of many villagers can be checked. Examination of these documents reveals that the 37 jurors in the 14 leets of the earlier series (1310–1334) were:

Holders of full or half lands and also reeves.	7
Other holders of full lands	7
Other holders of half lands	6
Cotlanders	5
Status unknown: bearing surnames of tenant families	4
Nothing known, but jurors only once	7
Nothing known, but juror only twice	1

and the 36 jurors in 49 courts of the later series (1362–1377) were:

Holders of full lands and reeves	5
Other holders of full lands	2
Holder of ¾ land and half land	1
Holders of half lands	13
Cotlander	1
Status unknown: bearing surnames of tenant families	7
Nothing known: jurors 18 and 37 times respectively	2

35

Nothing known: jurors 3, 5 and 6 times respectively 3
Nothing known: jurors only once 2

The investigation has shown that in the stable, earlier years, full-land holders probably constituted about half of the jury and half-land holders and cottagers made up the rest. In the later years in this much depopulated village the choice was necessarily limited and the reversal of the numbers of full-land holders with those of half-land holders does not necessarily signify a more liberal outlook in the choice of jurors.

VII. THE COURT: (2) THE LEET

The leet dealt with the assize of bread and ale, the affairs of the tithing, and lesser pleas of the crown (greater pleas having to go to higher courts). The offences under the assize have already been mentioned, the sins of the brewsters, the alewives and ale-tasters. The tithing actions concerned the failure of people to join tithings and the failure of the tithing men to take them as members: they also dealt with the harbouring of strangers, concealment of tithing offences and non-attendance at the leet. It is clear that these matters were all watched at Downham, for frequently one or two tithing offences were reported and on one occasion (4 December 1326) there were eleven offenders: five in no tithing, four neglectful tithing men and two who were amerced for harbouring persons in no tithing — one of these was a mother harbouring her two sons!

The lesser pleas of the crown included obstruction of the king's highway, obstruction of water courses by negligence or otherwise and the raising of false hue and cry. The watercourse offences occur often in the records: there were frequent single cases of offenders neglecting to clean their portions of the common ditches and, at the leet of 1326, eight were found to have neglected the ditch 'extending towards Grasshone': in December 1362 six had not cleaned the drain flowing below their holdings, and the following year one of these and five more had not done this work. Maybe the years 1362 and 1363 were unusually wet and floods were the result of the neglect?

Obstruction of the king's highway is recorded in five leets. In November 1311 eleven offenders had put dung heaps there and in December three years later two men had done the same. At the leet of 1367 John Benet was presented for having built a three-foot wall over part of the road and at the leets of 1369 and 1376 three men were up for having dug clay pits there and, worse, they had not filled them up. One other offender neglected to drain his osier bed and had thereby caused a flood on the highway.

There were just as many, and similar, offences in connection with the common way, by which was presumably meant, not the main road through the village, but the parallel roads running behind the houses and crofts on either side. These, too, were normally dealt with at the leet but there was one exception — the manorial court of 11 July 1365 dealt with obstruction of the common way at Downham Hythe: the manner of the obstruction is not stated.

False hue and cry cases were infrequent: only six are recorded, and the circumstances are never revealed. But 'rightful' hue and cry cases are also, without exception, heard at the leet and there are records of the hue being rightly raised twenty-nine times. Unfortunately, on no fewer than fifteen of these occasions the cause of the hue is not shown and no other entry in the roll for that day can be linked with it. For instance, on 23 November 1333 'Agnes the daughter of William Personn rightly raised hue on Hugo Kendale' but no misdoing of Hugo is reported.

The remaining fourteen cases, however, uncover a colourful aspect of village life. Margaret Dronneley committed *hamsoken* (house-breaking) against Robert le Honte, probably while he was out at work, for it was his wife, Joanna, who raised the hue. In 1363 Adam Miller raised a hue on Simon Chytom who had broken into his house.

In 1325 and again in 1331 some incidents suggest a feud between two village families, the Brewsters and the Columbers. In 1325 Juliana Brewster raised the hue on John Columbers and also on his son John. The elder John was amerced 3d. but there is no record of the nature of his offence: the younger John failed to turn up in court and an order was made to bring him to the next leet 'to answer to the said Juliana concerning an offence committed against the peace'. Six years later Joanna the wife of John Columbers and Juliana the wife of John Brewster each raised the hue on the other's husband and the families were at it again, enjoying another brawl. John Brewster was certainly a fighter: he was in trouble again in 1334 when he fought John Hayt and, more serious than bruising, 'drew blood' from him, causing Hayt to raise the hue. But another entry shows that John Hayt had drawn blood from Alicia Gardiner causing her to raise the hue on him so perhaps Brewster was after all justified in his attack.

Amicia, wife of William Stoneye, was another woman who got involved in brawls. Robert Stoneye drew blood from her and she raised the hue on him (1330 leet) and three years later she was the object of a hue herself for having drawn blood from Amicia Bronn's daughter, Isabell. Poor Isabell had to raise the hue the following year, but the cause is not reported: the villain of the story was one Alexander Scut, a member of a very respectable Downham family. Whatever he did cost him 3d.

Alicia Gardiner, Amicia Stoneye, Isabell Bronn – and yet another woman, Isabell Rous, was the victim of an attack (1363 leet). John Janyn drew blood from her: but she herself was up to something for Henry Taillour had to raise the hue on her; her misdemeanour is not reported but it cost her 6d. Meanwhile she raised the hue on John Janyn and that cost him a 6d. amercement.

Another woman who suffered 'drawing of blood' was Amicia Bathoke: John Kendale broke into her house and attacked her and it cost him 6d., John Taillour had raised the hue. John and Henry Taillour (the family came from Kersey) 'rightly' raised the hue three times in the 1360s and seemed to keep well out of trouble, but in 1373 Thomas Taylour seems to have been drawn into a fight with one Stephen Frost, a really troublesome character, and drew his blood, whereupon Agnes, Stephen's wife, raised the hue. This cost Thomas 9d.

The lesser pleas of the crown included hamsoken and of this there were six cases, five of which were causes of hue and cry. As usual the roll does not give the background story. Assault was not a lesser plea: although about two-thirds of the thirty-or-so cases did appear before the leet, the rest, just as serious, were dealt with in the manorial court. 'Defamation of character', too, was heard in either court.

The lesser pleas heard at the leet included offences already mentioned in connection with the keeping of the watch: in 1376 one man, and in 1363 four men, had failed to do this duty. The leet record of 1376 adds 'as ordered by the Statute of Winchester', which statute laid down rules, not only concerning the watch, but also about the holding of arms and ensuring that villagers spent their night inside, and strangers spent theirs outside, the vill. Another provision, seemingly rather out of step with the others, forbade the keeping of fairs and markets in churchyards: this is the only section that has not been repealed and remains in force to this day.

The recording of the leet proceedings, with those of the manorial court (the *curia*) which took place at the same time, generally follows a set pattern. The headings are usually 'Curia et Leta' or 'Curia et Visus Franciplegii', occasionally just 'Curia', the heading 'Leta' appearing lower down. The first part contains only *curia* matters. The second part, the leet report, contains, unexpectedly, both leet and *curia* work, even some purely village matters such as transfers of land. Before any presentations by the jurors are entered, however, there is a list of the twelve jurors and a record of the payment of the common fine of half a mark to the lord. Then follows a mixture of more leet and *curia* work, the assize of bread and ale, then more of the mixture as before, followed by tithing matters. Finally, very often, proceedings ended with one or two administrative village matters, such as the election of a hayward or an ale-taster. The lack of demarcation between leet cases and *curia* cases was a result of the fact that, as the bishop exercised jurisdiction in all of them, they were brought to whichever court was most convenient to him.

VIII. THE COURT: (3) THE *CURIA*

The *curia* had much to do: it had four separate functions:

    a. Dealing with presented offenders against the court, the lord and the community.

    b. Deciding pleas: pleas of debt, of covenant, of land and of trespass.

    c. Administration of village affairs.

    d. Transfer of lands and holdings.

Presented Offences

Offences against the court included that of failing to respond to a summons and that of making a false claim: both these wasted the time of the court. Offences against the lord were many and varied: damage to his crops, fences or lands; poaching and theft; refusing to do 'works'; failing to render suit to the mill (grinding corn at home); marrying without leave; withdrawal from the demesne, etc.

    Thefts were usually of such things as timber from the park or sedges from the barn but on one occasion three villeins were presented for stealing food: 'While carrying, on the lord's last return from Downham to Doddington, various victuals to the lord's kitchen at Doddington, the said John and the others took and absconded into the fen with fish and herring, they [the jurors] knew not how many. The jurors said that part of the said victuals thus concealed had been found, but part they had carried off, to the loss of, and in contempt of, the lord.'

    Offences against the community were mainly covered by the bylaw: they included selling sedges and turves outside the vill, cutting fodder on the common before midsummer and overloading the common pasture. The offence of selling 'lesch' (sedges) and turves was typical of such manors as Downham, with one foot in the fen. It must have been tempting indeed to cut more than was allowed for one's own thatching and fuel and for sale to one's neighbours.

    Offences against other villagers were sometimes presented but more often villeins had to bring their own complaints to get redress and damages.

Pleas

Pleas of debt   Money debts varied from ½d. to 36s. 8d. The halfpenny debt
(31 July 1314) was due from John Man, who was also guilty of 'malicious
words'. He appears as a debtor no less than ten times. But debts often consisted
of corn or peas, instead of money, which confirms, perhaps, the custom of
barter: there was 'corn worth 10d.' in one case; 2 bushels of corn and 4 bushels
of peas in another; two sheep in one case and a piglet in another. A few of the
pleas, though not many, have a background story. Some are claims for wages
and allowances: on 10 May 1330 Simon Cardinal sued William de Stoneye,
ex-reeve, for his wages, 12d., and his allowance of 2 bushels of corn: on 6
December 1330 Margaret de Coveney sued Simon Cardinal for her wages, 3s.,
for the previous year, 'and he could not deny this', and on the same day Henry
Corner sued Emma Scut for his wages of four years ago, 12d. The first and third
of these three cases went to inquest, the jurors finding each time in favour of the
plaintiff.

William de Stoneye was sued again on 19 July 1331, this time by Adam
Buk, for the sum of 36s. 8d. due from William 'on account of the agreement
made between them on the marriage of his [William's] daughter'. Actually,
Adam sued William for five marks (66s. 8d.): 36s. 8d. was allowed and he was
in mercy for his false claim for the rest.

On 10 May 1330 there was a case that is of interest on account of procedure. Roger King from Well sued Robert the chaplain of Downham 'concerning
the agreement made between them at Downham on the Monday next after the
Feast of the Assumption of Blessed Mary in the second year of the reign of the
present king: the aforesaid Roger was to carry from Well to Cambridge, for
8s. 5d., two thousand sedges; the said pence to be paid at Downham after
carriage was done. The said Roger carried the said sedges and sought the said
pence from the said Robert who . . . had unjustly kept it and still kept it.' Robert
disputed this, saying he had made no such agreement, 'nor was he withholding
a penny' and he would wage his law. A date was given to make his law four-
handed[1] at the next court. Unfortunately, at the next court, there was no sign
of Roger or of Robert and his four witnesses. No mention of the case appears
in that or in any later court.

This procedure of making law is recorded only three times in these papers:
the other two cases, one of making law four-handed, the other three-handed,
occurred in 1311.

Pleas of covenant   These, on the whole, make dull reading. In most cases the
inquest decided that there had, or had not, been a breach of covenant or agreement, and no background is given. In a few instances the facts emerge: on 30

1 with four witnesses.

June 1335 Emma de Soutere complained that Geoffrey the smith, to whom she had let a messuage for seven years, had, to her loss, 'allowed the buildings to go to ruin and had done repairs badly' and this although he had 'undertaken to maintain the buildings and walls of the said messuage in as good condition as that in which he received them'. The inquest found that Geoffrey had handed over the messuage in a better state, by four shillings, than that in which he had received it.

Another case, a complaint made by Ralph the carpenter against Ralph Eliot on 31 July 1314 is of interest only as an example of the procedure followed when a defendant in a civil case failed to appear: the court would not give judgment against an absentee.[2] In a 'personal' action (not one concerning land) the defendant was allowed three essoins: if he then failed to appear, he was summonsed: if he still failed, he was attached by pledges, then by better pledges; there was then an order to bring him bodily to court and after that, if he had not appeared, there was distraint of goods, first as a temporary measure and finally as a permanent one. In the case of Ralph Eliot, the case was adjourned at the first court; at the next (24 September 1314) an essoin was laid 'for the first time': on 17 December 1314 the case was again adjourned to the next court, 18 June 1315, when it was once more adjourned 'because the said Ralph had not been warned personally'. On 23 September 1315, the next court, the case is not mentioned but at the following one, 15 December 1315, another essoin is laid 'for the second time'. At the next court no mention is made of the case and then, unfortunately, six membranes are missing and the rest of the story is lost.

Another case illustrating the action of the court with an absent defendant concerned Simon le Barkere of Ely who was sued in a plea of trespass on 19 July 1331 by William of Bikleswade, sawyer (through his advocate, Alexander de Feltewelle). Simon was essoined at the three following courts for the first, second and third times. At the fourth court an order was made to attach him and to compel him, by distraint, to appear. This order is repeated and reported to be 'in process' at the fifth court, but after this brisk application of the law nothing more of the case is heard, though the records continue without a break. No appearance is recorded, no further order, no 'leave to agree', no note of withdrawal.

Pleas of land   One land dispute (between Geoffrey Morris and Geoffrey Smith) has been described already.[3] Two others are of interest because in both cases the issue was decided by scrutiny of the rolls. Janyn Columbers (14 December 1322) pleaded that Simon Cardinal 'had kept him from posses-

2 F. Pollock and F.W. Maitland, *The History of English Law*, 2nd edn. (Cambridge, 1968) Vol. 2, pp. 593–4.
3 Chapter III.

sion of half a messuage belonging to his half of the land'. Simon denied this, saying that 'he had deforced him of no messuage nor half of any messuage, and that he said this because he had paid half the gersuma in the time of the lord William of Routh and in evidence of this he called for the record of the roll at that time. Therefore an order was made to examine the rolls of the time of the said William.' The upshot of this was that at the next court Janyn Columbers was amerced for 'false clamour' (false claim) against Simon.

The other case decided by scrutiny of the roll was one concerning Agnes the widow of Philip Lovechild. She was his second wife: there was a son William of the first marriage. William had a half land and a messuage in Downham and Agnes claimed this (13 December 1329) as her dower 'because it had once belonged to Philip her husband'. William disputed this, saying that the holding had once belonged to William Dumfrey and Amicia his wife who 'at the court held on the Thursday next after the Feast of St Andrew the Apostle, in the twentieth year of the reign of King Edward son of King Edward' had surrendered it to the lord for the benefit of William son of Philip Lovechild, and he, William, had taken the tenement from the lord and had paid ingress money, 20s. He asked for a copy of the transcript of enrolment 'and goes to the rolls for his warrant'. The roll proved him to be right: the tenement had never belonged to his father.

One dispute led to confiscation of the land in question because the defendant, John Curteys, failed to turn up in court, in spite of three summonses, to answer to Simon Jecup (21 July 1374). 'The hayward was ordered that the said land be taken into the lord's hand for view, etc., and a day [was given] for leasing it.' This illustrates the different processes in 'real' actions concerning land and 'personal' actions concerning chattels. John Curteys was sent three formal summonses and when he still did not answer them his land was confiscated. It was, however, a temporary measure: he could reclaim it after a fortnight if the custom of the manor followed the law on this point.[4]

Pleas of trespass A trespass was 'a wrong done to the plaintiff in his body, his goods or his land'[5] and it therefore covered a variety of offences. Many cases of assault make their first appearances as inquest decisions and must have been brought by pleas. Several were of beating, others of 'roughly dragging' (31 July 1314), 'treading on' (23 September 1315) – 'John Hayt trod on Simon Cardinal to his hurt' and that cost John 6d. for damages. On the same date there was 'drawing blood' and, on 10 September 1331, 'dragging and scratching'.

Theft (unless of the lord's goods or covered by the bylaw) was dealt with under a plea. On 15 December 1315 is recorded the theft of John le Sumencer's blue cloth tunic worth 2s. by Thomas of the hythe whose sword, also worth

4 Pollock and Maitland, *English Law,* Vol. 2, p. 593n.
5 Pollock and Maitland, *England Law*, Vol. 2, p. 526.

2s., was stolen by John le Sumencer. There were also cases of poaching fish and one, prophetic of a custom of today, of borrowing a boat without leave.

One unusual case appears on 24 February 1328, a case of 'entering' but not 'breaking into' a house. 'Robert, the clerk and mainpast of Robert del Brok, chaplain, entered into the house of Clement the brewster against the wish of Clement and took some wool into that house and there disposed of it. Wherefore the said Clement received from his neighbours disgrace and reviling words to his damage, assessed at 2s., which the court considered he should get from the said Robert, chaplain.' Presumably the chaplain or his clerk was making it appear that Clement had stolen the wool but, as usual, the story is incomplete.

Only two months earlier, this Robert del Brock had been the object of attack by Amicia Pope who had 'falsely and maliciously shocked and defamed' him and had 'brawled outside the house of John Sinerles to the damage of this Robert'. There were other cases of defamation of character, malicious words, and of slander (22 September 1311): 'Alice the wife of Clement the brewster with her husband, likewise, complains about William le Fefere in a plea of trespass because on the Thursday next after the feast of St James the Apostle recently past he slandered her by accusing her that Proud Hugo ought to have acknowledged her to his loss, etc., and afterwards in full court, solemnly, he [Proud Hugo] came three-handed and cleared himself of the offence'. So such offences as slander were also covered by the term trespass.

Another plea of trespass that must have brought some human interest into that day's proceedings was heard on 12 June 1312, when Henry Corner lodged a complaint against John the brewster. 'Because it was found that the said John ... had committed adultery with the said Henry's wife and was not able to keep away from her the said Henry often waylaid the said John so that the great risk might not come about. It was considered [by the court] that henceforth the said John must not have any association with the said Henry's wife and must not be with her in any place, neither in the church nor in the market, under pain of paying half a mark to the lord and forty pence to the said Henry, etc. None the less, he will be punished for the trespass.'

This attitude of the court, preventing future trouble, is echoed in a case the following year (13 December 1313) when a 'devastator of the common fen', William the feoffee, after complaints from many people, was put into the care of the rector of Downham: anyone harbouring him did so under pain of 20s. payable to the lord.

Attorneys A word about attorneys. The privilege of doing suit of court by attorney was granted to every freeman by the Statute of Merton in 1236. In Downham there are records of two attorneys. One was Alexander de Feltewelle, who acted for Alicia Kebbe (5 June 1333) in the matter of her dower, and, as already mentioned, for William of Biggleswade, a sawyer who was the plaintiff in a plea of trespass on 14 July 1331 and on 29 May 1332. The other was William de Burgh, attorney to the prior of Ely: he appeared four times in court to lay essoins on the prior's behalf.

Another unusual legal point was the reference of a case to the lord's council. This concerned the burning of the fen (13 March 1376: see Chapter IV).

Administration of Village Affairs

Election of officers and general supervision of village affairs were the normal duties of the court but the troubles of the later years provided it with new problems: the management or filling of the vacant holdings, the repair of dilapidated cottages, the tracing of fugitives. Little is heard of dilapidated cottages in the early, more prosperous, days: only one order to do repairs, one order to produce a pledge that repairs would be done and two orders for distraint for failing to comply. But from 1362 there was constant trouble.

John Kendal had neglected his cotland in 1365 and was distrained of two of his cows until he should satisfy the court that he would do his repairs. (Unfortunately for the reeve, the cows escaped!) Richard Lacy was presented 'by the homage' on 20 September 1369 because his half land had deteriorated through neglect: the loss was assessed at half a mark. He produced pledges, the rector and Simon atte Townesend, and was given until Easter to put the place in order. But in no time, by Michaelmas, he had 'withdrawn from the demesne' and the rector was landed with the property and its burdens. He was relieved of this, however, by Thomas Skut for whom also he stood pledge.

Margaret Pope, on 4 March 1374, was distrained of a calf and a sheep before she produced her pledges, but Rosa Stoneye who, on the same day, was ordered to produce pledges, kept the court occupied on every law day until, on 13 March 1376, her holding, having 'fallen into ruin' was 'taken into the lord's hand'. No one was found willing to repair the place for her, and it must have properly tumbled down for the last heard of it is that an order was made that such of her timber as could not be used for rebuilding should 'be put in a certain place from where it may be sold at the best price by the reeve and from where it may be possible to load it'. This order about timber was shared by another unfortunate, John Cook, whose case had cropped up on every law day in 1376 and whose lands, also, had been confiscated. The reeve had charge of the confiscated lands and was responsible for their profits.

Alan Draper and John Janyn were two more in trouble, before every court in 1374, 1375 and 1376, failing to produce pledges. Finally an order was made to seize their goods and chattels, whereupon Alan managed to find pledges but poor John Janyn did not, and as he had 'neither goods nor chattels as witnessed by the lord's homage' his holding had to be confiscated.

The first record of fugitives is in March 1362 when four villeins had 'withdrawn from the manor'; one more went in 1370. Four disappeared in July

1376 and the court gave orders, in successive courts, for their tracing and capture, but they were still abroad in February 1377. The whole homage was expected to help trace a fugitive, the hayward was ordered to attach him, and the reeve to keep him in custody until the next court.

Three other matters occupied the time of the court, all concerning the stock. First, the trespassing animals, the horses, cows and pigs that damaged the crops. They were impounded and, until they were collected by their owners, were kept by the reeve who reported the matter to the court. The owner was charged a penny for every animal in poundage. This could be quite profitable: 44 beasts in the corn brought 3s. 8d. on 28 March 1365, and on 23 July 1366 it was reported that 53 heifers had been impounded. These numbers were unusual: it was more often about four or five animals that found their way into the crops.

The strays were another matter. Their owners were not known, so their descriptions were reported in court by the jurors and they were put into the reeve's charge until they were claimed by their owners who had to produce proof of ownership in court.

Then, thirdly, there was the 'murrain'. Frequent cases of sudden death were occurring among the animals, diminishing and impoverishing the stock. Every such incident had to be reported to the court, and also the cause of death, whether it was the 'murrain' or neglect by the stockman. These sad entries are frequent: twenty-one courts between 1365 and 1377 report sudden deaths. The victims included one carthorse, 10 mares, eight foals; three oxen, 22 cows, two heifers and five calves; one boar, one sow, 11 pigs and 27 piglets. The epidemic seems to have been at its height in Downham in 1370: on 30 May that year nineteen sudden deaths were reported from the lord's stock alone and some, also, from the tenants' animals. On one occasion 17 January 1365, the roll tells of the sudden death of a mare, a colt and a filly, presumably the lord's, but this time the cause was not murrain but 'poor custody', and the keeper was answerable. The object of the regular report, therefore, was not only to follow the course of the 'murrain' but to keep a watchful eye on the stockman.

Transfer of Lands and Holdings (Tables X and XV)

Every transfer had to be made through the court, otherwise it was illegal and the action was void. Thus, on the death of a tenant his heir came to court and 'sought admittance' to his land; to effect a sale of land the tenant came to court and 'surrendered it into the hand of the lord for the benefit of' the purchaser who was then admitted into it.

This ritual is recorded 167 times in the 136 courts examined in this study: family transfers were made in 44 cases, 123 transfers being alienations:

	Earlier series of rolls	Later series of rolls
Family transfers		
Customary holdings and cotlands	29	2
River meadows and fisheries	3	3
Houses	1	nil
Parcels of land	4	2
	37	7
Lands alienated		
Customary holdings and cotlands	21	15
River meadows and fisheries (and new fisheries, 4)	11	6
Houses	5	2
Parcels of land	43	20
	80	43

On admittance to land the tenant paid a tax, a 'gersuma', as 'entry money'. If he was succeeding to a full land or a half land on the death of the former tenant he paid the death duty, heriot, the rate of which was fixed by custom of the manor. The jury of 7 Jury 1328 brought the attention of the court to the rule of heriot: consequently the details are set out in the record for that day. (the best beast or 32d. for a full land and half that sum for a half land). The amount of 'gersuma', however, followed no definite rule and varies, for instance, from 40s. to 6s. 8d. for a half land in the earlier years and from 13s. 4d. to 6d. for a cottage. In the earlier years, with the 117 transfers, there were few excusals of 'gersuma', but in the later period, with 50 transfers, there were 28 excusals. Ten of these were for tenants taking up vacant lands and unwilling to do so, six were for tenants taking up land from the demesne, and six were excusals for reasons unstated.

Every transaction with its accompanying payments was recorded in the roll: it was thus that the tenant obtained his copyhold, his proof of ownership, and it was not worth his while, in order to evade the payment of 'gersuma', to buy land without the leave of the court.

IX. INHERITANCE AND DOWER

By the year 1272 one of the features of the law of inheritance was that 'males exclude females of equal degree: among males of equal degree only the eldest inherits: females of equal degree inherit together as co-heiresses'.[1]

The law of dower, arrived at by the fourteenth century after various changes, ruled that a widow 'was entitled to one-third of the lands of which her husband was seised at any time during the marriage'; this was her 'common law dower'.[2]

These laws of inheritance and dower, however, governed the disposal of the lands of freeholders, not those of villeins who were subject, in this matter, not to common law but to 'the custom of the manor'. It is interesting to see, from what happened to the Downham lands on the death of a villein, what the custom of the manor was — what a widow would receive as her dower, whether the eldest son was the heir without question or whether the land could be alienated by sale or gift to someone outside the family. The information is derived from the twenty-five cases that are recorded, among other land transfers, in the court rolls (Table XV).

Fourteen of these cases concern the succession of a son or a daughter on the death of the father. Ten of them are quite straightforward but four are of interest:

William Brewster (3 December 1327) had parted during his lifetime with seven acres of land and part of a messuage to Simon Pope, who held it in villeinage: when William died, however, his son John came to court and claimed the land and the messuage and they were granted to him.

Simon Dovey held a messuage which he pledged to William Brewster to pay for a quarter of corn 'on a certain day agreed between them on which day the said Simon did not pay' for the corn. So William held the messuage, and after two years he handed it over to his son Clement who passed it back to him to hold for the rest of his life. When Simon Dovey died, his son John made his claim to the messuage: and the inquest found that as William, who had also died 'recently', had entered the messuage only by Simon's pledge and not by payment in court, he had held the land in error. And John Dovey was admitted to it (6 March 1332).

Simon Scut died and his eldest son, Philip, was 'living at a distance' so the

---

1 Pollock and Maitland, *English Law*, Vol. 2, p. 260.
2 Pollock and Miatland, *English Law*, Vol. 2, p. 421.

second son, Nicholas, was admitted to the half land and he took it 'reserving the right of it to Philip' (24 February 1328). Nicholas died and the land passed to the third son, Geoffrey, under the same conditions. Geoffrey surrendered it to John the son of Geoffrey the smith of Downham, who took it on the same terms. Finally, Philip came home and was admitted to the land (11 September 1329). Incidentally, he then surrendered it to the said John who undertook to give Philip, for the duration of Philip's life, 4½ quarters of corn a year.

The fourth case is that of Adam son of Peter of the hythe who left a half land to his widow Amicia and a half land to his daughter Isabel. Amicia remarried and kept her land: Isabel surrendered her half land for her mother and stepfather, Hugo the shepherd, as part of a maintenance arrangement whereby Isabel would receive annually a quarter of wheat, 1½ quarters of barley and half a quarter of peas.

In every one of the ten straightforward cases the son or daughter is described as 'his son and nearest heir', 'his son and heir', 'his daughter, his next heir' or 'his daughter, to hold for herself and her family ... according to the custom of the manor'. It was clear, therefore, that a son or daughter should succeed and John Brewster had no difficulty in obtaining his father's holding although his father had, during his lifetime, parted with it to Simon Pope. He did not even have to have an inquest about the legality of the earlier transaction: he was the son and he was admitted to the land. It was different in the John Dovey case. He claimed his father's land which, like John Brewster's, had been alienated by his father, and he was admitted to it, but not before an inquest had found that the previous transaction had been made 'without payment in court'. He was not automatically admitted as a son; he was admitted because his father's alienation of the land had been illegal and therefore void. It seems, therefore, that although it was the custom of the manor for a son or daughter to succeed (and the Scut case stresses that the *eldest* son was the rightful heir) yet there is an implication in the Dovey case that sometimes the custom was 'bent' and the land could be alienated.

Three other cases (one of five acres in 1312, two of full lands in 1328 and 1332) all concern sons succeeding on the death of their widowed mothers, and one case, a full land in 1328, was of a grandson's succeeding his widowed grandmother. In these four instances, therefore, the widow must have inherited. It may be, as suggested for common law cases,[3] that she was left with infant children and was the most competent person to become the tenant.

There are five straightforward cases, also, of the widow succeeding: in 1329 William Personn died and his full land, half land and cotland all went to his widow Juliana, to hold as long as she remained unmarried; and in 1334 Henry Sauser died and his quarter land and cotland went to his widow Alice 'for the duration of her life'. The three other widows held the land even after they had

3 Pollock and Maitland, *English Law*, Vol. 2, p. 437.

remarried: Robert the carter died and left a messuage and a virgate of land (a full land) 'with appurtenances' to his widow Alice who still had the right to it after her second marriage, with Robert Russell (another carter). This case is first mentioned on 17 December 1314 when it had been the subject of an inquest and was referred to as Alice's 'dower' from her late husband. The land was now held jointly by Alice and Robert Russell and was being transferred by them both to Simon Pope who handed it back to them to hold for their lives. Simon son of Thomas left 'a piece of land' to his wife Agnes who later married Robert Moriz: on 2 March 1368 an inquest found that it was being 'wrongfully kept' by William Veal and his wife, for on the death of Simon it ought to have passed to Robert and Agnes to hold for their lives. And Simon Kede (16 March 1362) left a half land and a cotland to his wife Caterina who later married Simon Rote and was able, with him, to keep her land. It is not stated whether, in these five instances, there were children too young to manage the lands or whether there were no children to inherit, but it should perhaps be assumed that one or other was the case. It is noted that only one of these widows held the land with the restriction on remarriage: a second marriage, ensuring a man in charge of the holding, had obvious advantages.

Two claims for dower are reported: they both suggest that the one-third rule was normally regarded as binding. Nicholas the reeve died in 1304. His widow Alice had agreed (presumably 'at the church door') to accept as her dower one and a half acres from his four-acre holding – just over the customary one-third. She turned up in court in 1310 and claimed against Ralph Eliot for the remaining two and a half acres, but Ralph quoted her agreement of 1304, pointing out that six years had elapsed since then, perhaps referring to an allowed limit of 'a year and a day' in which to make an appeal. The case was referred for inquest and adjourned until the bailiff was in court, and at the next court her appeal was refused and she was amerced 3d. for false claim.

The other case concerns Alicia, widow of Richard Kebbe who was 'man' to William Personn, to whom Richard had sold his cotland and house and two acres of land. When Richard died Alicia claimed (26 June 1324) her dower from the cotland and house, but William maintained that the sale of the land to him had been made with Alicia's assent, and he asked for an inquest. The inquest was held and Alicia admitted on oath that 'hitherto on the death of their husbands' widows 'were not accustomed to be endowed with a tenement'. So she lost her claim. However, on 5 June 1333, nine years later, she returned to the charge – this time with an attorney, Alexander de Feltewelle – and appealed once more for her dower, one-third of the cotland and one rood of the land 'according to the custom of the manor'. This time she was successful, the attorney having presumably managed to correct the wrong statement she had made to the inquest about the custom of the manor. It would be interesting to know the substance of his plea: perhaps the sale of the land turned out to have been illegal, 'without payment in court', or perhaps it transpired that when Alicia had consented to the sale she had not been properly examined on the matter and had not understood what was afoot.

The rolls also record some 'family arrangements' made by tenants for the disposal of their lands after their death. In these cases the land was formally transferred to the heir and formally handed back by him for the tenant to hold 'for life': the land to revert to the heir on the tenant's death. Five of these have been found: Agnes Bridge and her son John (25 February 1311) transferred her half land to a younger son William; Simon Cardinal (16 December 1325) his half land to his son Geoffrey; John Cok (30 June 1335) his half land to his daughter Isabell; Robert Aleyn and his wife Isabella with their son Nincolas (30 June 1335) their cotland to their daughter Emma; John Kebbe (17 December 1314) a quarter land, a cotland, a messuage and an acre to his brother Richard who handed back the cotland and part of the messuage and part of the acre adjoining it, for John to keep until he died; it would then revert to Richard. The law of primogeniture seems to be underlined in two of these cases: John Bridge, the elder son in one family, and Nicholas Aleyn, the son in another, both took part in the formal transfer of the land. It is just possible that partnership existed between John Bridge and his mother Agnes and between Nicholas Aleyn and his parents, and that their consent was needed on that account. It seems more probable, however, that the presence of the sons in court was essential because they were the heirs and their parents could not dispose of the land without their permission.

Two other tenants made different arrangements for the disposal of their land. On 10 September 1331 Christiana Bathoke handed over to Hugo Kendale, her son by a former marriage, her cotland and house, and he granted her a room in the house for life and, every Michaelmas, two bushels of wheat and two bushels of beans. Agnes Rote handed to her son John a cotland and a half and an acre and a half, and he granted her, for life, a 'house with some land'.

There is an example of an unconditional transfer of land in the case of the Virli family. Alexander Virli's first wife, Margaret, had a cotland in her own right. She died, leaving it to her son William, but he must not succeed until the death of his father Alexander – the only case in these papers of 'the curtesy of England'. Alexander remarried and, on 23 September 1315, William formally surrendered 'his entire right and claim' to the cotland for the benefit of his father, his stepmother Agnes and their daughter Agnes: 'thus let him keep no right or claim in the aforesaid cotland nor can he demand it or lay legal claim to it, for ever'. A similar unconditional transfer took place on 20 September 1335 when Isabella, widow of Simon Buk, handed her full land, with a messuage, to her son John.

Before leaving this matter of family land transfer, there are three early cases of men 'marrying into' the land. Hugo, son of Nicholas the shepherd, obtained leave in 1315 to marry Amicia the widow of Adam, son of Peter of the hythe, and 'enter her holding', a half land. John Buk 'entered' the full land of another widow, Agnes, widow of Adam the carpenter, in 1316. And in 1315, Hugh son of John the carter had leave to marry Amicia the daughter of Clement Stot who handed his cotland over to them. One might expect the 'gersuma' to be greater than usual in these cases and John Buk did have to pay £1 for his entry into a full land whereas another full land, about a year earlier, had changed hands for half a mark. But the 'gersuma' rates were inconsistent and unpredictable: to enter Amicia's half land Hugo paid only half a mark which was the rate paid for entry into a half land in 1311; but in 1312 the 'gersuma' for a half land with a house was as much as £1.

Besides the family 'arrangements' for transfer of land there are a few similar cases in which the transfer is not a family matter. The case of Robert the carter and Alice his wife has already been mentioned: they sold a full land to Simon Pope, who handed it back to them for their lives. Richard Eliot (21 October 1322) surrendered a messuage and six acres for Richard Kede: Richard Eliot to keep for his life two acres only of it and some meadow, and to give Richard Kede 200 sedges and 500 turves a year and also all the dung from his share. Robert the chaplain, son of Richard le Keu (23 September 1332) surrendered for Robert, son of William Stoneye, a messuage: the chaplain was to hold it for his life, paying six marks to Robert Stoneye in acknowledgment of the holding: and afterwards it would revert to Robert Stoneye.

Wills

There are references in the court rolls to the executors of four testators: they all occur in the earlier series of rolls and they all concern debts. It is unfortunate that the registration of wills did not begin until more than a hundred years after these wills were made and it is only when the villagers buy or sell land, pay or collect their debts in court, that anything can be learned of their circumstances.

The executors of Nicholas Scut first appear on 24 February 1328, the day on which 'Geoffrey Scut, villein of the lord, came here to court after the death of Nicholas Scut his brother': the story of the Scuts' land has been told above. The executors were Emma the widow, Thomas de Weston, Master of the Hospital of St John, John de Walcot and John Cok. The roll of 22 April 1328 shows that the executors owed Simon son of William Personn 1½ quarters of barley worth 5s.: William of Stoneye the same amount of barley and 4s. in money: and Adam Buk 36s. 8d. On the other hand various tenants, including William Personn and Simon Cardinal, owed the executors various amounts of barley and money, totalling 14s. 4d. Further, Nicholas had made arrangements with Robert the carter, William Personn and Simon Kede to pay them, on three future dates, barley and money to the value of 5s., 5s. 8d. and 2s.

Simon Pope's executors (Margaret his widow, Simon Buk and Geoffrey Scut) turn up on the same day, 24 February 1328, in mercy for much the same debts: to William of Stoneye 8s. and 1½ quarters of corn worth 5s.; and two others, 3s. and 1s.

Clement Brewster's executors, John Columbers and his son, appear on 6 March 1332, the day that John Dovey (mentioned earlier as claiming his father's land) said that Clement, who had held it, had 'recently died'. There was a plea of debt against the executors but it was not pursued. Finally, the roll records, of Simon Buk's estate, that on 20 January 1334 his executors sued Robert the smith for 40d.

X. THE CROPS

Apart from occasional references in the court rolls to trespass or to damage by stock there is no record of the crops grown by the tenants. As, however, the arable land of the demesne lay with the customary lands in strips in the three fields, the tenants' cropping programme must have been, to a great extent, that of the demesne, and one can but use the reeve's accounts as a guide to the agriculture of the vill.

Table XI shows the acreage allotted, year by year, to the various crops grown on the demesne. It will be seen that the main crops were wheat and barley (malt was needed in quantity for beer): peas and beans, full of protein, came next — these were introduced in Downham at any rate by 1318. Rye normally covered a much smaller area and occasionally was not sown at all. Except in two early years, the oats crop, needed for fodder, was also given very small acreage and oats had to be bought for demesne use.

Although there are records of the demesne sowings for twenty-nine years, yield figures can be obtained for only twelve. The produce of a crop was not entered in the grain account until it had been threshed and could be reckoned in quarters and bushels, and it therefore appears in the account for the year following that in which it was harvested. To arrive at the yield figure, therefore, one must have two consecutive accounts and in these papers this fortunate incident happens only twelve times (Table XVI).

With the figures obtainable for so few years it is perhaps unwise to accept them as at all indicative of the state of farming in Downham, or to attempt any sort of comparison with the published figures of other manors. For what it is worth, however, some comparison has been made between the Downham figures in Table XVI and the yield per seed figures for the Winchester estates[1] and also those for the Ramsey estates.[2]

The Winchester statistics deal with 41 manors, and comparison is possible with the figures for eight years for barley (1318, 1330, 1341—43, 1345—47), for seven of these years for wheat and oats and for four of them for rye. The Winchester yields varied considerably from place to place, the manors being situated on many types of land. Taking first the wheat, for which the Winchester figures usually varied from 1 to 5: three of the seven years, 1318, 1330 and 1345, were very good years for Winchester, with many yields of over 4, some over 5 and

1 J.Z. Titow, *'Winchester Yields'* (Cambridge, 1972).
2 J.A. Raftis, *'The Estates of Ramsey Abbey'* (Toronto, 1957).

(3) The east end of the fourteenth century chancel of Downham church.
Photo: Leonore Hoke

(4) The south doorway of Downham church (twelfth/thirteenth century).

Photo: Simon Lamb

more; and in these years the Downham yields (in spite of the good harvest there in 1318) were only equal to those of the very least productive of the Winchester manors. In the other four years, however, 27 or 28 of Winchester's manors were yielding between 2 and 4, against Downham's similar results.

Oats, in the Hampshire manors, produced steady crops, usually varying from 1 to 3. The Downham figures, on the other hand, fluctuate considerably, being higher than nearly all of Winchester's in 1318, 1343 and 1346 and lower than nearly all of them in 1330, 1341–2 and 1345.

The Downham barley crops were consistently good, the figures for 1346 and 1347 being higher than nearly all those for Winchester (which varied, most years, from 1 to 6) and the figures for the other years coming about one-third of the way down the Winchester list. As for rye, only three Winchester manors were interested in this, but their yields were consistently high, about 3 to 5, much higher than those for Downham.

The Ramsey figures (Table XVII) can be compared for only two years for wheat and oats and four years for legumes and barley. Their manor of Warboys was on exceptionally good, well-tilled land and its yields of every crop well exceeded those of Downham. Compared with the other manors, however, Downham did well.

It will be seen from Table XVI that, although all crops were sown in 1344/45 as usual, no harvest is recorded for any crop for the autumn of 1345. Tables XVIII and XIX echo this: no sales of any corn are recorded for the following year, 1345/46. No sales are recorded either for the years 1336/37 and 1361/62, and though there are no accounts for the preceding years 1335/36 and 1360/61, it can be assumed that no harvests were recorded for them. These years were all vacancy years, years in which occurred the death or translation of a bishop and the arrival of his successor. John Hotham died in 1337, his successor in 1345 and the next bishop in 1361. During the vacancies the king held regalian rights; that is to say, he could appropriate the revenues of the bishopric, including the feudal dues, the advowsons of benefices in the bishop's gift and, what is concerned here, the corn and stock and profits of the bishop's demesnes. Keepers were put in charge to administer the estate.

During the bishopric of John Hotham, however, Edward III issued an order[3] that in future, during the vacancies in the Ely bishopric, the prior and convent should have the custody and the 'temporalities', except for the feudal dues and the presentation of benefices. After John Hotham's death, therefore, and during subsequent vacancies, it was the prior and convent who adminstered the estate and appropriated the profits, keeping the lands tilled and the demesnes equipped to hand back to the incoming bishop when he had done homage to the king. A copy of the order appears as Appendix III.

---

3 *Fine Rolls*: 2 March 1329: 1327–37, pp. 120, 121.

XI. THE STOCK

It has been seen how, during the vacancy periods of the bishopric, the cultivation of the demesne was carried on by the priory. Sowing and reaping were done and the land was tilled but, as far as the stock was concerned, only those animals that were essential for the cultivation of the land were kept. The dairy cows and the pigs were sold, and so were any horses and oxen that were not needed for carting or ploughing. The profits of the sale went to the lord (or, in the case of his death, to his executors) and the new lord, when he took possession, had to build the stock up again.

Thus there appears in the stock account for the year 1344/45 (in which year Simon of Montacute died on 20 June) the sale of 6 mares; 2 bulls, 30 cows, 7 bullocks, 5 heifers and 12 calves; a boar, 2 sows, 21 pigs and 22 piglets; 1 carcase, 1 pelt, 2 hides; 3 capons, 9 hens and 50 eggs. This left no stock whatever except the 2 carthorses, 4 stots and 15 oxen required for agricultural work. The finance account for that year corresponds exactly, showing that the mares were sold at 13s. 4d. each, one bull and the 30 cows at 8s. 6d. (the other bull with 2 bullocks and 2 heifers were grouped in the account and made 30s. altogether). The 5 other bullocks and the 2 other heifers sold at 3s. 4d.; all the calves sold at 1s. 6d. Curiously, the boar and the sows sold for only 1s. 8d. each, as did 9 of the pigs and 3 of the piglets, but the 12 other pigs sold at 2s. and the 19 other piglets at 8d. The carcase and hides made 4s. 11d. Capons sold at 2d. each, hens at 1½d.; eggs were 50 for 2d. The profits from the sale came to £24. 6s. 7d.

As this is the only Downham account that illustrates the clearance on the event of a vacancy, some accounts for Wisbech Barton have also been examined. The one for the year 1373/74 (during the vacancy after the death of John Barnet) shows a complete clearance of stock (even including the oxen, every one of which fetched either 21s. or 18s. 5d.). Here the prices were higher than they had been thirty years previously at Downham: one mare went for 16s., the boars for 2s. 6d. and 1s. 10d., a sow for 1s. 10d. The pigs, however, fetched only 1s. 6d. each, though the piglets were 1s. 1d. (There was no dairy herd at Wisbech Barton, but they kept, and accounted for, a flock of sheep normally about 200–350 ewes and 4–18 rams.)

The Downham stock account for the year 1345/46 shows some building up of the stock by the new bishop: 18 mares are collected from other manors. Pigs are reintroduced the following year, but there is no sign of a dairy herd until 1348, after which time the numbers are normal.

To return to the draught animals which were there throughout occupation and vacancy. Up to 1351/52, when 140–180 acres were being cultivated by the demesne, there were always two cart-horses, four or more stots and about 17 oxen. From 1363/64 (after the gap in the accounts) when only about 120 acres were being cropped in the demesne there were no stots and fewer oxen, and the number of cart-horses increased to three, and finally four. Ploughing was normally done by oxen and stots: a plough team consisted of 'six oxen and two stots, according to the custom of the vill' (1251 extent). The cart-horses were kept for the heavy carrying work and some of their journeys were long. Consequently they were given extra provender − four quarters of oats each from Michaelmas to Lammas: this works out to half a peck a night and none on Sunday! It is interesting to compare this with Walter of Henley's advice on the feeding of horses: 'He ought to have at least every nyght [from 18 October to 3 May] the sexte part of a bushel of oats.[1] The Downham cart-horses had an equivalent of one-eighth of a bushel on six nights out of seven but their ration continued for three months longer than that of Henley's horses.

Brood mares appear in the stock accounts in the early 1320s: there were often four or five mares with foals. But there are no more until the year 1343/44, when seven mares arrived from Ely and five foals were born. Six of these mares and the foals were sold the following year after the death of Bishop Simon of Montacute and the seventh was sent to the Lady Prioress of Haliwell. The year 1346/47, in the time of Bishop Thomas de l'Isle, begins with 18 mares and for six years there are almost continuous records of breeding, with 10–18 mares producing six or seven foals a year − possibly 12 in one year when six were born at Downham and six mares were sent to Somersham 'before foaling'. Presumably the stallion was then at Somersham: he is not recorded as a resident at Downham until 1348/49 when he was 'received at Michaelmas' and John atte Wood, keeper of the stallion, was paid 2d. a day for twelve weeks to take charge of him. Incidentally, the shoeing of this horse cost 10d. The stallion appears, as well he should, at the head of the stock lists in 1350/51 and the following year, and the grain accounts show that he was given three pecks of oats every night from midsummer to Lammas 1350 and one peck a night from Lammas to 'the Saturday before the Feast of the Conversion of St Paul' which would be 22 January 1351, during which time he was 'living here'. William Coltman was now the 'keeper of the stallions and mares at stud' in receipt of 2d. a day.

For the last ten years of the episcopate of Thomas de l'Isle there are no accounts, but in 1361/62, the year after the following vacancy, there was one mare, and there were from three to seven thereafter.

The dairy herd usually consisted of about 20–25 cows and as a rule every

---

1 D. Oschinsky, *'Walter of Henley and Other Treatises on Estate Management and Accounting'* (Oxford, 1971)

cow produced a calf.[2] There were disastrous years: in 1319/20 14 cows and 18 calves died and in 1348/49 12 cows died, seven of them in calf. In many years the cows were farmed out: there is evidence of this occurring fifteen times between 1322 and 1370. The tenant took, at Michaelmas, all the cows and all the heifers that had calved: in the early years he paid 4s. a cow, then 5s., and later 5s. 6d., and half these amounts for the heifers. The following Michaelmas he would receive a quarter of corn. The lord was to have, in the early years, all the calves, but by 1330 he took only the best ten. Later, he shared the calves equally with the tenant, taking 'every other one' and finally in 1368/69 the tenant had 29 cows but only six calves were to go to the lord.

The court record of 4 December 1326 shows that not only the cows were farmed out that year to Robert Hasteler: the cows were farmed out for the whole year but from Michaelmas to Easter all the other animals, even the cart-horses and the plough teams, were taken over by him. No reason for this is given in the roll and none is evident: this was not a vacancy year – it was in the middle of John Hotham's episcopate. The reeve's account shows the farm of the cows but makes no reference to that of the rest of the stock.

After the bull and the cows, the bullocks, the heifers and the calves come the boar, the sows (generally two), the pigs and the piglets (as a rule between 40 and 80 pigs and piglets). About 30 were born nearly every year and the piglets seemed to do pretty well. There was one bad year when out of the 30 born 15 died, but this was very unusual and more often than not they all survived to pig-hood. One-tenth of those born were given away annually in tithe: three piglets were an almost regular payment.

After the pigs came, latterly, the three capons and, throughout, the 59 hens (64 less the five excused for the reeve, hayward and smith) which had been paid as rent by the tenants. Those not needed for consumption were entered as sold. No other ordinary poultry is recorded. There were geese, however: in 1321/22 one goose was bought for 4d. and 12 were sold at that price, and in 1330/31 records mention them in the fen in charge of a goose-boy – but they do not appear in the accounts again. One year, 1345/46, seven swans are recorded: they were all given away.

The account rolls tell of a dovecot: extensive repairs were done to it in 1343/44 and the following year; it was not until after that that it was stocked with pigeons, 66 in one year, 94 in another and so on, until 1352. They must have been a valuable source of food for 'the lord's larder' and that was where they all went except for some that were given as livery and the tenths that were paid in tithe. In 1347/48 a peacock and peahen appear in the stock account and the following year there is a pea-chick, but in 1350/51 no more were

2 That is, according to the reeve's account: but, as M.J. Stephenson pointed out to me, the reeve, held liable for all losses and shortages in cash, grain and stock, may sometimes have entered the number of stock expected to be born in a healthy herd rather than the actual number born.

hatched 'because there was no mating' and the family disappears from the records.

A good source of food supply was the warren with its rabbits and even these were entered in the stock account when they were sent to the lord's other manors (Somersham in 1331/32) or when they were sold, 33 in 1367/68 and 20 the following year. They were sold for 2d. each so were not a cheap article of food and it is not surprising to find that Robert Page, caught snaring rabbits in the park in 1363, was amerced as much as a shilling. This is the only case of rabbit poaching found in these papers; presumably the large amercements made it not worth while. In 1312 the parson's 'hunting dog' was seen chasing the lord's rabbits and pheasants 'to their great hurt' but it seems that he failed to catch any, for the court case ended in a warning!

The vast industry of the sheep and the wool was centralized in many of the great estates and this was to some extent the case with the bishop's manors. It is not possible to say to what extent this was done for there are reeve's accounts for only two manors, Wisbech Barton and Downham. The Wisbech Barton stock accounts record year by year the numbers of rams and ewes, hoggets, lambs and fleeces, and the money accounts record the purchases and sales. Clearly, therefore, the Wisbech Barton fold was administered by an officer of that manor, The Downham stock accounts, on the other hand, contain no reference whatever to sheep; nor do the money accounts bear any entries concerning sheep or fleeces. Clearly, therefore, the fold was managed elsewhere, even if some of the lord's sheep lay in Downham

The Downham money accounts record the payment of a shepherd's wages of 5s. every year from 1301 to 1375, and also regular payments for hurdles (usually between 40 and 60 a year, from Cambridge, at 1s. 4d. to 2s. a dozen plus 3d. or 4d. for carriage to Ely by water). This does not necessarily show that the lord's fold contained any of his own sheep, for the shepherd may well have been employed, and the hurdles used, wholly for the sheep of the cottagers. Two entries in the money account, however, are of interest: they concern transport of 38 sheep in 1344/45, and 33 wethers in 1348/49, from Hadstock to Downham, and this suggests that the lord did keep some sheep in the Downham fold. This was certainly the case at the time of the 1251 extent which tells of 'two hundred sheep reckoned by the long hundred which, together with the cottars' sheep, must lie in the lord's fold'.

The flocks of the villagers are, of course, not recorded and the only clues about their size are the entries in the court rolls of presentments for two offences, keeping sheep outside the lord's fold (this would refer only to cottagers) and damaging crops or trespassing. Many of these entries omit the numbers of sheep involved and even those that supply the numbers are by no means conclusive for all of these villagers may have owned many more sheep than those involved in the offences. For what they are worth, however, the figures (arranged in order of flock size) in the earlier series of court rolls are:

Cottagers with sheep outside the lord's fold

	No. of sheep	Date
Adam Buk	50	December 1325
Geoffrey Scut	40	December 1325
Philip Lovechild	15	December 1325
Simon Buk	10	September 1311
Simon Pope	10	September 1311
William Personn	10	September 1311
William of Stoneye	10	September 1311
Walter Brond	10	July 1331
Richard, son of Alan	9	April 1326
William and Thomas Brancaster	8	July 1331
John Columbers	1	April 1326
John, son of John Cok	1	April 1326
William of Hotham	1	April 1326
Simon Sauser	1 and 1 lamb	April 1326

Cottagers with sheep damaging crops, etc.

	No. of sheep	Date
Adam Buk	80	July 1330
Adam Buk	40	1 August 1334, September 1335
Adam Buk	12 and 30 lambs	July 1330
Geoffrey Scut	50	1 August 1334
Geoffrey Scut	20	July 1330
Simon Buk	40	July 1330

Customary tenants with sheep damaging crops, etc.

	No. of sheep	Date
Richard Buk	40	September 1335
John Cok	30	July 1330
Simon Cardinal	30	July 1330
William Scut	4	July 1330
Geoffrey Cardinal	4	July 1330

In the later series of rolls the status of the tenant is not always known, but the offenders were:

	No. of sheep	Date
John Benet	100	December 1362
Nicholas, son of Simon	40	December 1362
Nicholas, son of Simon	40 and 12 ewes	May 1369
Geoffrey Buk	40	May 1369
Geoffrey Cardinal	40	May 1369
John de Stoneye	40	May 1369
Katerina Cardinal	40	December 1362
John Wrong	20	December 1362
John Lovechild	12	May 1369
Simon Rote	12	May 1370
John Koc	8	May 1369
John Buk	6	November 1375

An entry in the court roll of 20 May 1327 concerns an enterprising cottager, Geoffrey Scut, who, having bought ten acres of free land from the prior of Ely, asked leave to keep 'a fold of a hundred sheep reckoned by the long hundred (120) on the said land'. Another cottager, Adam Buk, made a similar request on 5 December 1328: he had bought eight acres from the prior. Their petitions were granted provided that they did not let into their folds any sheep, ewes or lambs of other cottagers, for those must lie in the lord's fold. They could keep their folds, as long as it pleased the lord, by villein tenure at 2s. a year payable at the four usual seasons. They each paid 10s. for the permission. Scut kept his fold until 1344/45 and Buk until 1348/49: by 1350/51 they had both died.

About the rest of the village stock: most of the customary tenants must have had some draught animals for the cultivation of their holdings and for the ploughing which they owed to the lord. A few may have had the full plough-team of 'six oxen and two stots, according to the custom of the vill' (1251 extent) but many would have fewer draught animals than this and some would have none.

One family, the Bridges, were, it seems, by way of being dairy farmers: Geoffrey Bridge, in April 1368, had a bull doing damage in the lord's meadow: in July 1366 Thomas Bridge had 21 trespassing cows and, in September of that year, 12 heifers. Although the rolls record no other such large numbers of cows (only of Simon Sinerles with three in June 1363 and of John Ducat with four in September the following year), yet the numbers of young stock found trespassing (John Tame's 12 bullocks in 1368, John Pypeshank's 12 heifers in 1379 and the eight heifers of William Dean in 1363 and of William Deye in 1373) suggest that several of the tenants had small herds. All the above instances are from the records of the years after 1362, which also tell of two tenants with two cows each and five with one, one tenant with four heifers and six with three, and thirty tenants with one or two heifers or bullocks. The records for the earlier years, before 1335, reveal only one tenant with a good number of stock – Robert the son of Isabel of Coveney had 20 heifers trespassing in September 1330. Otherwise, John Hayt had three cows in September 1332, three others had two in June 1329 and one tenant had one. Nine tenants had two heifers and one had one. From all this it can be assumed that practically every tenant had at least one or two cows, and several must have had small herds. The size of a herd must have been limited by the rules concerning the over-stocking of common land but there is nothing more in the records to help with their numbers.

A little is learned, too, from complaints of damage to crops, about the pig population. These cases reveal that one tenant, the rector of Downham (James de Columbariis), kept a boar in September 1328 and that Nicholas Scut had ten pigs in December 1326, Simon Pope had eight the previous December, Geoffrey Smith six and John Cok five. William Stoneye had four in August 1326. Also in these early years, four other tenants had three trespassing pigs, ten had two and thirteen had one, while twelve more tenants had an unstated number. In the records of the later years the rector, Thomas Amies, had 24 pigs. Three tenants (Rosa de Stoneye and Richard Buk in December 1362 and John Swift in November 1368) had four pigs. There were also two tenants with three pigs, four with two and six with one.

This wandering population of cows and pigs on the common and in the woods needed herdsmen and two of these are recorded, John Hayt and William Chephird. There only remains to mention the geese and the poultry. Many villagers probably kept geese; they are mentioned three times: William Stoneye with eight, William Personn and Matilda Starling with six in 1327; and, four years later, Reginald Kede with six. All the tenants kept poultry and had to give two hens (or, in two cases, a capon) to the lord at Christmas and eggs at Easter as part rent for their holdings.

XII. BIOGRAPHIES OF SOME VILLAGERS

There is enough information in the rolls about several of the villagers to enable one to form some idea of them as individuals and to construct some very sketchy biographies. The records show what property a man owned and what office, if any, he held in vill or in court. They often show what work he did and what was his status. As in the media of today much is recorded of misdemeanours while there is no note of the uneventful life of a law-abiding villager — 'the good is oft interred with their bones'.

Three groups of people are first described in these biographies: the rectors, the chaplains and the freemen. Then a number are dealt with in families: first, three sheep-owing families and then seven others. Four, the Buks, the Cardinals, the Kedes, the Stoneyes, were old village families: their names appear in the list of customary tenants in 1251; Stoneye appears in 1222. After the families come seven individual members of the community who are, for one reason or another, of interest. Only their nearest relations are mentioned.

In the family groups there is sometimes difficulty about identity. If a name recurs at intervals throughout a period of about sixty years it may refer to one man or it may refer to (say) a father in the earlier years and later to his son — though normally the latter would be known as 'son of' his father. In these biographies it has generally been assumed that the name belonged to one man only and that a septuagenarian, though perhaps rare, was not unknown.

The Rectors

The earlier series of rolls mentions the rectors many times but never by name. A list in Downham Church, however, supplies the names of all the rectors from 1274:

1274:	Albert de Alneto
1294:	Geoffrey de Kingston
1298:	James de Columbariis
1338:	Robert de Cotty
1352:	Thomas Amys (named in the later rolls)
1379:	John Quye

and the Calendar of Patent Rolls shows that in 1267 *William de Swaffham* was Rector of Downham: on 10 March of that year he was granted protection for one year 'on condition that he stand his trial if the King or other will proceed against him'. Read with an entry of 5 March 1267, a royal order to deal with a revolt in the Isle of Ely (see note on p. 1), this suggests that William had been involved in some rebellious action.

James de Columbariis was a sporting parson who owned a hunting dog that chased the lord's rabbits and pheasants 'to their great hurt' and was 'wont to do damage in the lord's meadow', but when James was presented in March 1312 the court let him off with a warning. In June 1312 he sent two of his household into the park with a bullock's carcase: they dragged it into a ditch where it attracted dogs, and the dogs disturbed 'the beasts of the chase to the lord's loss'. This time the rector was amerced £1. In December 1315 he was presented for cutting a hundred bundles of osiers in the lord's osier bed: the amercement was 2s. He was presented on three further occasions, each time for doing damage with his pigs: four in the lord's crops (September 1314), some in Katharine the hayward's corn (December 1324) and a boar in the lord's corn (September 1328); all this suggests an interest in pig farming. One entry – on 13 December 1313 – records that a village ne'er-do-well, William the Feoffee, a 'devastator of the common fen' and a man whom to 'harbour' was to do so under pain of 20s., was put in the care of the parson. This shows the rector in another light, the social worker or probation officer of his time.

Thomas Amies certainly went in for pigs: twenty-four did damage in the lord's park (September 1362) and the following September he paid 2s. for pannage for twelve piglets. At the same court he paid 2s. for the agistment of four colts. At the court of 7 October 1367 he took up 6½ acres of demesne land 'lying against the rectory' to hold from Michaelmas 1367 for 'six years' (an error for eight years) at 1s. an acre: the rent to be paid at the four usual times a year in equal parts. The accounts for 1367/68 and 1368/69 show the payment of rent, the former stating that the lease was for eight years and the latter that seven years remained. There is no account for 1369/70 but there is a rent roll for that year which records that the parson of Downham rented 6½ acres 'abutting on the south side of the church in the cultura called Churchill at 1s. an acre' (Appendix I). So the rectory was beside the church then, as the present Old Rectory is today. There were two more presentments: one in July 1365 for taking an ash tree from another man's holding and selling it; for this Thomas was amerced 6d. In July 1369 he had, without leave, exchanged a rood of land with Adam Kede, and this cost him 3s.

On 20 September 1369 he stood pledge for Richard Lacy, one of the unfortunate villagers whose holding had deteriorated through neglect and who now undertook to 'repair, maintain and improve' it. He was given until Easter to do the repairs on pain of half a mark. Richard, far from getting his holding in order by Easter, 'withdrew from the manor' at Michaelmas, leaving the place 'entirely abandoned' and in the hands of his unlucky pledge. However, on 4 March 1370, the rector managed to dispose of it and it was taken by William Scut, to hold for life.

The Chaplains

The chaplains of Downham were, successively, the lord's chaplains. *Adam* is the first mentioned in the rolls and all that is known of him (February 1311) is his 'great offence against the wife of Robert Allen' and his false complaint of Robert, which makes a bad beginning.

Robert del Brook followed Adam and held the chaplaincy from 1312 to 1332. He was a cottager (presented in May 1330 for withdrawing seven sheep from the lord's fold). Emma, the wife of Nicholas Scut, was his sister: in September 1327 she and Nicholas sold to him, or probably gave him, a river meadow and in March 1332 a parcel of villein land 33 x 53 ft. lying next to land that Robert already held.

Robert was thus very much a man of Downham and throughout he joined in the life of the village and did his share of quarrelling. In his early days (1314) Simon Cardinal's son 'drew his blood' and in May 1330 Robert beat and maltreated Simon to the tune of 12d. damages. Before that, in January 1326, he had had to sue Simon for 35s. and a bushel of wheat. Amicia Pope seems to have had something against him for she 'falsely and maliciously shocked and defamed' him and brawled outside the house of John Sinerles to Robert's damage (December 1327). Two months later Thomas Pope (as pledge for Clement the Brewster) was having to pay Robert a debt of 16d. Perhaps there was a link between these two incidents and another that was reported in the latter court (February 1328): Robert's mainpast, or dependent, Robert the clerk, 'entered into the house of Clement the Brewster against the wish of Clement' taking some wool into the house and there disposing of it, 'wherefore the said Clement received from his neighbours disgrace and reviling words to his damage assessed at 2s.' which Robert the chaplain had to pay. It is difficult to understand just what was happening here: had Robert the clerk stolen the wool? and was he, with the chaplain's connivance, 'planting' it on Clement to persuade the neighbours that it was he, Clement, who was the thief? It would be interesting to know more.

Another story about Robert concerns the plea of debt brought against him by Roger King for payment for transport of sedges, Robert's threat to wage his law four-handed and Roger's capitulation (May 1330).

Another villager made a false claim against Robert in December 1330. Henry Corner accused him of owing an unstated sum but the inquest found that he owed 'not a penny'. The same day, however, he stood pledge for his sister Emma who, also, was being sued by Henry Corner — for his wages (12d.) due four years previously. She denied the debt but this time the inquest ruled in Henry's favour.

Robert was presented for a few other offences, the most serious being his cutting of 1000 sedges in the fen before Michaelmas, 'thereby doing much damage'. The reason he gave was the 'weather was fine': perhaps he wanted to get his sedge-cutting done before winter set in. The following year (December 1315) he got his boy-servant to steal three sheaves of the lord's corn for him, another instance of Robert's getting the members of his household to 'do his dirty work'.

It is surprising to find, in June 1324 and in December 1330, during Robert's time, the name of two other chaplains, *Master John* and *Nicholas de Caldecote*. This John was falsely accused by Clement Brewster of having 'kept (for himself) 2d. out of the 31d. which was handed to him from the collection of the levy of the Holy Ghost'. Nicholas received payment of a debt, 4 bushels of corn, from the executors of Simon Cardinal.

The Freemen

The extents of 1222 and 1251 note four free tenants:

1. The *Prior of Ely* who held 120 acres of land, sub-let to the *Fulk* family (son of Ivo Fulk in 1222 and Clement son of John Fulk in 1251). By 1328, 18 of these acres had been sold to villeins.
2. *Thomas the chaplain* who held 28 acres for 3s. a year. By 1251 he had acquired, also, 46 acres of assarted land 'in Bindingfold in Apesholt' for 3s. 10d. a year.

    The Fulks and Thomas all owed boon-work to the lord: they had to go themselves to the harvest and take four men with them: all of them were given food.
3. *Ralph de Leyton* (Longtown) in 1222 (*Giles of Longtown* in 1251) who held 7 acres for 1s. 6d.
4. *Roger le Grand* in 1222 (*the Hospital of St John of Ely* in 1251) who held 3½ acres. Their services included digging in the lord's vineyard, working on the Aldreth causeway (doing a length of 15 feet or paying 2d.) and putting up the lord's messengers when they came to Downham. They owed suit of court but the Masters of the Hospital were reluctant to attend, often defaulting or paying 2s. 6d. for a year's exemption.

Simon Keten is the only other freeman named in the rolls as such. The inquest of 17 May 1329 showed that he had bought, six years earlier, two acres of land from Richard Kede. In December 1332 it is recorded that he had exchanged, with Geoffrey Skut, five acres of land in the Downham fields for five in the Ely fields. He had, also, an alder grove: on 21 October 1322 he asked for an inquest to decide the damages due to him on account of the felling of a tree there by five lads. Damages had been assessed by the court at 2s. 4d. but apparently Simon considered this inadequate. When he wanted to complain that two villagers, John of Wereham and Roger Wyset, had gates leading on to his land the case was not brought by Simon himself as a plea of trespass but was presented by the jury, an unusual procedure. Those lands of John and Roger were free lands and no action was taken (December 1315). One debt is recorded:

Simon, together with Simon Cardinal, owed 6d. 'which they paid annually' to Anota atte hythe, but in what capacity she worked for them is not revealed (December 1330).[1]

Families

THE SCUTS

Simon Scut held a half land. He had three sons, Philip, Nicholas and Geoffrey and when he died he left the half land to Philip, his eldest son and heir. Philip was 'living at a distance', so Nicholas was admitted to the land and he took it 'reserving the right of it to Philip'. When Nicholas died, the land went, under the same conditions, to Geoffrey, who immediately disposed of it similarly to John the son of Geoffrey the smith of Downham, who surrendered it to Philip on his return.

Philip Scut, the eldest of Simon's three sons, claimed the family half land at last in September 1329 when an inquest revealed the whole story of the inheritance. He at once let the land to John, son of Geoffrey the smith, for 2 quarters of wheat, 2 quarters of barley and half a quarter of peas and beans a year, payable equally at four seasons.

Nicholas Scut, Simon's second son, held no sort of office and was not a juror, which is curious, for he must have been a man of some standing, being one of the few who are known to have left a will. His only land transactions were the rentings for four harvests of one acre from Simon Kede and one acre from John Child, both in February 1327; and, in September the same year, the sale (or gift) of a river meadow from himself and *Emma his wife* to her brother, Robert Brook the chaplain. Other entries about Nicholas mainly concern damage done to crops by his sheep and other stock and debts due to him collected by his executors after his death. The numbers of sheep are only given once – there were 12 in the lord's corn in December 1326. The debts due to him are interesting in that though some were in cash, many were in barley. They were dealt with by his executors in the court of April 1328:

Due from	William Personn	5s. and 2 quarters of barley worth 8s.
	,, ,,	1 quarter of barley worth 4s.
	Robert the carter	5s.
	Simon Kede	½ quarter of barley worth 2s.

1 Two other people can be assumed to have been freemen because of their employment of attorneys: Alicia Kebbe and William of Biggleswade (see Chapter VIII).

Henry Sauser	3s. 6d. for 6 bushels of barley	
	and 1s. 6d.	
Richard Dumfrey	1s. 8d.	
Simon Cardinal		1 quarter of barley worth 2s.

Some of these were being claimed prematurely by the executors, who were amerced accordingly.

And Nicholas owed:

to Simon, son of William Personn		1½ quarters of barley worth 5s.
Adam Buk	36s. 8d.	
William of Stoneye		4s. and 1½ quarters of barley.

all of which the executors admitted. *Emma, widow of Nicholas*, told the court that she had received all the goods and chattels that were due to her on her husband's death. She claimed, and was paid, the sum of 32s. 8d. which she had spent since his death in settling some of his debts. The executors were Emma the widow, Thomas de Weston, Master of the Hospital of St John the Baptist of Ely, John de Walcot and John Cok.

Geoffrey Scut was the youngest of Simon's three sons. When his turn came to take possession of the family half land he at once parted with it (February 1328) to John the son of Geoffrey the smith of Downham. He was therefore not a customary tenant and had to keep his sheep, of which he had a considerable number, in the lord's fold.

On 20 May 1327 he appeared in court and asked leave to keep a fold of a 'long hundred' (120) sheep on ten acres of free land that he had bought from the Prior of Ely. He was granted permission to 'farm a fold over the said land' provided that he did not let into it any of the other 'customary sheep, ewes or lambs which must lie in the lord's fold'. The fold was to be held by Geoffrey 'as long as it pleased the lord' by villein tenure of 2s. a year payable at the four usual seasons. He paid 10s. for the permission.

Geoffrey made other land transactions, besides his purchase of the ten acres: in February 1327 he had rented an acre from Hugo the shepherd for three harvests; in May 1329 an inquest found that he had bought 3¾ acres from 'a freeman' and in July 1331 another inquest found that, again from a freeman, he had bought 9¼ acres. In September 1329 he sold an acre and a ditch to Thomas of Hotham. In December 1332 he exchanged with Simon de Keten five acres in the fields of Ely for five in the fields of Downham. In July 1331 he bought a fishery (Nelisdam) from Richard Kede.

Geoffrey was elected a custodian of the bylaw in 1314 and again in 1325; in 1328 he was keeper of the warren, a custodian of the vill and a custodian of the new ditch. He appears as a juror at twelve leets in the earlier series of rolls.

Many of his presentments in court concerned sheep: in December 1325 he had had 40 in Simon Pope's fold, in December 1328 and again in July 1330 he had kept 20 beyond the permitted 120 in his own fold. In December 1330 he had depastured sheep on the stubble among the clover and in September 1331 60 of his sheep had damaged the lord's corn. On 1 August 1334 he had had 50 sheep (presumably additional to his 120) outside the lord's fold. In his early days he tended to be slightly antisocial, cutting fodder on the common before St John the Baptist's Day which was 'against the ruling about the seasons' (July 1311); eight others were presented with him for this offence; the others were all amerced 1s. or 6d. but it cost Geoffrey 2s. and he was also amerced 3d. for contempt. In December 1313 he was presented, with his brother Nicholas, for digging on the common land at Downham Hythe. He was once (September 1311) in trouble for bad reaping and before he bought his own fishery he poached with a fish-trap in the lord's Berton Dam (July 1328). Four debts are recorded, early ones of 2s. 1¼d., 1s. 6d. and 11d. and a later one of 4s. to Emma, his brother Nicholas's wife.

He died some time between 1345 and 1351. The reeve's account for 1344/45 is in three parts, due to the death of the lord (Simon of Montacute) on 20 June 1345 and the arrival of the new lord (Thomas de L'Isle) on 10 September 1345. The first part, to June 1345, shows that Geoffrey had paid the 2s. for his farm of fold for that year: the second part (the vacancy period) is missing: the third part has an entry 'the other fold, formerly [let] to Geoffrey Scut was not farmed'. The next year's account, 1345/46, also says 'Geoffrey Scut has not the other fold of sheep' — it does not say that he had died: the 1350/51 account reads 'nothing from farm of fold this year because the tenants have died.' Geoffrey had also at some time farmed a fishery, and the 'Farm of Fisheries' section of the reeve's account for 1344/45 shows that 'the new ditch towards Littleport, half a fishery, which Geoffrey Scut held, is in the hand of the lord for lack of a tenant'. All this suggests that he became ill during 1344/45 and died between Michaelmas 1346 and Michaelmas 1350.

There were a few more villagers with this name but it is not possible to trace their kinship, if any, with Simon and his three sons. Two women, *Matilda* and *Agnes,* have trivial mention — the former grazed cows on her neighbour's pasture and the latter rented from John Man half an acre for three harvests, without leave. There was another *Simon Scut* who, five years after the death of his name-sake, was helping himself to three sheaves of corn in the harvest of 1333, and there was his father, *William,* custodian of the bylaw and of the vill and, in December 1329, resigning from the office of hayward at the cost of 6d. This William's date of birth could not have been later than about 1300 (assuming that the corn-stealing son was born in or before 1320), but it is possible, though not probable, that he was the same as a rebellious *William* who appears in the later series of rolls, from 1368 to 1376. This one was a juror in two courts in 1376 and also a custodian of the bylaw. His first entries (in the later series) are in May 1368 when the jurors presented that another villager, John Rote, had 'held him so that he was hit' and in November 1368 when they presented that John Frost had 'drawn blood' from William who had rightly raised hue against him. He continued to have a rough time of it the following year, when he was elected (made) to take up a vacant cotland for which no one else wanted to be responsible. However, six months later (March 1370) he took over, 'for twelve years or for life' another holding, a half land which had been badly neglected by Richard Lacy who had 'withdrawn from the manor' leaving it 'entirely abandoned'. William was to pay 12s. a year, render all services and keep the place in good order. His pledges were the Rector and John Wrong.

In July 1376, however, the court changed the conditions of this tenancy: instead of paying rent William was to hold the land by services and dues entirely. He quite rightly refused, in that court and the next, to agree to this arrangement and finally, in December 1376, he was ordered by the steward to comply. But he had put up a good fight.

THE BUKS

Adam Buk, like Geoffrey Scut, was interested in sheep and, not being a customary tenant, had to keep them in the lord's fold. With Geoffrey he was presented in December 1325 for having 50 sheep in Simon Pope's fold and for this he was amerced 18d. Also, like Geoffrey, he bought land fron the prior of Ely (8 acres in his case) and applied for leave to farm on it a 'long hundred' (120) sheep. This request was granted on 5 December 1328, provided that he let into the fold no other customary sheep, ewes or lambs that must lie in the lord's fold. He was to pay 2s. a year at the four usual seasons and to have the fold as long as it pleased the lord. He paid 10s. for the permission. He kept the fold until his death in 1348/49 or 1349/50. The 1349/50 account is missing but that for 1350/51 records 'no farm of fold: both tenants having died'.

Adam had other land. Inquests were held and their findings reported in May 1329 and July 1331, concerning the purchase of free land by villeins, and these disclosed that in the earlier year Adam had bought five acres from a freeman and in the later year, 5½ acres from Thomas Thine, a freeman. For the 5½ acres a rent was arranged (the amount was on part of the membrane which has been torn away) and Adam had to render a due, a hen at Christmas. Earlier, in February 1327, Adam had rented, for four harvests, 3 roods of land from Simon Warren: and an acre from John Man and half an acre from Hugo Shepherd, both for three harvests. All this renting had been done without leave, but the transactions were regularized by entry in the roll and on Adam's paying the appropriate fines, 4d., 3d. and 3d.

He married in 1331 one of the daughters of William of Stoneye and there was a little argument about the money due from William on the marriage. The amount agreed was twelve marks: Adam sued William for five saying that only seven had been paid. An inquest found that only 36s. 8d. remained unpaid: William was in mercy for this debt and Adam for his false claim.

As in Geoffrey's case, most of Adam's misdoings concerned his sheep. One very early presentment did not: he was presented in October 1324, with five others, for damaging Emma Pope's wall. After that it was all sheep: in July 1330 he had 12 sheep and 30 lambs (over the allowed 120) in his fold, and he had crossed the lord's meadow with 80 sheep. On 1 August 1334 he was amerced for having 40 sheep outside the lord's fold, and in September 1335 for having 40 sheep doing damage in the lord's wheat – this was a double offence for they were also 'outside the fold' and the amercement was 12d.

Simon Buk, a customary tenant with a full land, belonged to the generation before Adam and may have been his father, though Adam is never referred to as his son. He was a regular juror for many years, missing no recorded leet from 1311 to 1329. He was elected a custodian of the bylaw in 1314 and a keeper of the warren in 1328. In 1324 he was an assessor of taxes for arms: the taxes were assessed, like the rates of today, on the value of the holdings and in three cases he overcharged the tenants and they lodged complaints in court.

He was reeve from Michaelmas 1326 to some date in 1331/32 when, probably because of illness, he handed over to Geoffrey Cardinal.

There are records of two early land transactions: in May 1314 he exchanged, with Simon Cardinal, half an acre of meadow 'in Parrok' for half an acre 'above Barleydonehone', and in February 1327 he rented, without leave, five roods of land for three harvests from Hugo Shepherd.

Apart from his misdeeds over the taxes little ill is known of him: bad reaping in 1311, a small debt (2s. 1½d.) the following year, breaking the assize, as a brewer, in 1325 and one offence with sheep: in 1330 he allowed 40 to cross the lord's meadow.

He died before 11 May 1334: in the court of that date his executors claimed a debt of 40d. from Robert the smith. He left a widow, *Isabella*, and certainly one son, Richard (who succeeded to the full land in September 1355, on his mother's death) and possible Adam also. Richard and Adam were both Simon's executors.

Richard Buk, a customary tenant, was a juror in three leets (1322, 1333 and 1334): he was elected a custodian of the vill in 1328 and a custodian of the bylaw in 1334. He had sheep: 40 strayed into the lord's corn (September 1335). He had two sons, Richard and Robert.

The two sons, *Richard junior* and *Robert,* were not a successful pair. Richard had a half land, presumably his half of his father's full land, and by March 1362 it was on the list of vacant lands and Richard had disappeared. Robert possibly had the other half of his father's full land but this does not appear in the existing

records. Anyway, he too absconded and in July 1376 both brothers were reputed to be living in Fordham and the whole homage were ordered to assist in
finding and arresting them 'bodily'. These orders continued through 1376 and
1377 with no result. So much for the family of Richard son of Simon.

Back in the earlier years *another Robert,* a contemporary of Simon
(possibly his brother), was presented for bad harvest work in 1310 and was a
defaulting brewer in 1314; he was a juror once, in the leet of 1315. He had a full
land which he left to *Agnes,* one of his two daughters, who took it up in May
1325 and sold half of it to Simon Sauser. Later that year, without leave, she
married Richard Aleyn. Robert's other daughter, *Joanna,* also married without
leave, in 1334. Her husband was John, son of Nicholas Morris.

There were a few more villagers named Buk but one cannot say that they
were related to the foregoing. Another *Agnes Buk* and a *Margarita Buk* appear
in 1331 and 1334 leets, respectively, as defaulting brewsters (this Agnes was not
the same as Robert's daughter Agnes, for by 1331 the latter had become Agnes
Aleyn). There was a *John Buk* who married the widow of Adam the carpenter
and entered her full land (February 1316); he died in the year 1348/49 and his
heriot was an ox.

Beatrice Buk, known as Beaty Buk and sometimes Baldy Buk, was another
in the early years. She was a defaulting brewster, presented with monotonous
regularity at every leet except two from 1310 to 1334 – for breaking the assize
of ale. Her ale must have been awful, or perhaps she just did not take the trouble
to send for the ale-taster, or put up the sign that she had just finished brewing.

Still further back, listed in the 1251 extent as holding a half share in a full
land, was *Wolmar Buk,* who was perhaps the grandfather of Simon or, indeed, an
ancestor of all or any of the Buks in the village.

There remain two villagers of the later years: *John Buk II* and *Geoffrey
Buk,* both cottagers. This John was a juror twice in 1373 and three times in
1376 and also a custodian of the bylaw. He rented the Manea fishery for 2s. a
year and had some sheep – he was presented in 1375 for having 6 of them
outside the lord's fold.

Geoffrey Buk was a juror at every recorded court (except two) from
1362 to 1377. He was elected hayward, with John of Stoneye, in 1370 and
custodian of the fen in 1373. The rent roll of 1369/70 shows him as having an
acre of demesne land near the mill, at 1s. 4d. an acre. For the year 1373/74 he
rented an acre of demesne land 'in Middlehallcroft' at 1s. an acre, and two acres
in 'Over Holmhone' at 1s. an acre; and the following year he renewed the lease of
one acre. All this was for the purpose of growing corn: this is specifically stated
in the roll.

He gave trouble now and then, gathering corn badly in the harvest of
1363, failing to keep watch in the November of that year, defaulting in suit of

mill in 1364 and 1365. In 1368, because he failed to do his services and pay his dues, his beasts were impounded: he then 'broke the pound' and got them back -- for that he was presented and amerced 6d. The following year he kept 40 sheep outside the lord's fold from Hokeday to May and they all got into the lord's barley: these offences cost him 2s. In September 1369 he was elected by the whole homage to hold a half land which had been left vacant by the death of John Deye in 1361 and had been passed from one tenant to another ever since. He was excused the payment of gersuma on entering, being 'unwilling to take up the land'. But he had to hold it by services and dues according to the custom of the manor.

THE POPES

Simon Pope appears in the documents from 1301 to 1327, the year of his death. He was a customary tenant: he acquired a full land and a house from Robert the carter in December 1314 and handed it back to Robert and his wife for the duration of their lives; it would then revert to Simon. Meanwhile he held for the duration of his own life 'three-quarters of a messuage' and a full land which he was renting from William Brewster and which was to revert to the Brewster family on Simon's death. By the time Simon died William Brewster, also, had died, and John Brewster his son claimed the land in February 1327. Simon held, also, a cotland and two roods of land, 'one in Snakeland and the other at Hankele', together with part of a certain dam in the fen, and all these he passed to his son Thomas in June 1324. He made three other land transactions: in July 1311 he bought a river meadow from Juliana the gardener, in February 1311 he sold a plot of land (3 x 1½ perches) to John de Personn and in December 1325 he sold an enclosed piece of land (4 x 4 perches) to John de Columbers.

He had a sheep fold: on one occasion (December 1325) it was found that the sheep of three cottagers were lying there – sheep that should have been in the lord's fold. They numbered 15, 40 and 50, so Simon's land would benefit from their stay, but it was the cottagers who were presented and amerced; beyond aiding and abetting, Simon had committed no offence.

He was reeve in the year 1300/01 (his name appears in the heading of the accounts), a juror at five of the six recorded leets between 1311 and 1325, was elected a warden of the bylaw in 1311 and again in 1325, a warden of the fen in 1326 and an affeerer in four courts shortly before his death.

He was in trouble in court twice: in December 1315 for cutting 100 bundles of osiers in the lord's osier-bed, and the following February for taking, from a negligent swineherd, a fine already collected by William Personn, the reeve. In what capacity Simon was acting is not told: for each of these offences he was amerced 2s.

Simon was substantial enough to leave a will: his executors were his widow *Margaret*, Simon Buk and Geoffrey Scut. His son Thomas already had his cotland. To Margaret he left the full land which he had bought from Robert the carter and his wife Alice and which he had passed back to them for their lives. He left a few small debts: one of 8s., one of 3s. and one for corn worth 5s. Margaret did some brewing during Simon's life-time and was four times presented for breaking the assize. She re-married in 1328: in the July of that year Reginald, son of Richard Kede, asked the lord's leave to marry her and enter her holding: he paid 20s. for the permission.

His son *Thomas* must have been a respected member of the community for he was a juror at every recorded leet from 1311 to 1334, a custodian of the bylaw once and an ale-taster six times. His misdemeanours included breaking down, with five other villagers, part of the park fence (all the others were amerced 6d. but he, for some reason, was pardoned), and breaking the assize of ale three times, as a brewer. His wife, *Agnes,* exceeded this figure: she was found to be a defaulting brewster in eight leets between 1311 and 1332. But she must not be confused with another *Agnes Pope, Alewife,* who sold bread and beer contrary to the assize in 1324. This Agnes was held to be of evil repute and an order was given 'to remove her'. However, she was back in the village by 1327, beating another woman, Anota Bron.

There may be some link between Simon and *Emma Pope,* whose marital status is not given: perhaps she was his sister. Her wall 'next to the holding of Simon Pope' was damaged in 1324 by five villagers who were still being ordered to repair it six months later. There are four more shafts of light on Emma: in 1315 she appears as a regrater of bread; in 1322 she 'did damage to the lord's house and sold timber from there to the value of 6d.'; in the same year she suffered harassment from Geoffrey the smith, who was ordered to pay damages of 6d. and 'to remain peacefully at home'. In June 1329 she had two houses on 'a parcel of land', both badly roofed; the roofs were to be repaired by Christmas.

Two less colourful Popes were *Isabel* and her son *Adam*: she died in 1312, leaving him five acres of land and a house. Another, *Katharine Pope,* was a defaulting brewster nearly every year from 1311 to 1328. And there was *Amicia Pope* who falsely and maliciously shocked and defamed the chaplain, Robert Brook, and brawled in the village street (1327). There was *John Pope* who owned part of a cotland: he was found taking corn at harvest in 1324, and in 1322 he not only 'defamed Joanna, the wife of Robert Hunt, calling her a thief' but also falsely accused her of defaming him. Years later (1376) he had 'withdrawn from the manor' and was reputed to be at Fordham and throughout that year and the next the whole homage were ordered to help to find and arrest him.

In the later series of rolls there is also another *Margaret Pope* who was in real trouble over the dilapidated state of her house and plot of land. For six years efforts were made to get her to do her repairs and eventually orders were given to distrain first a cow and calf and finally all her goods and chattels.

It is well to remember that a villager who was not able to take up any office in the vill and who neither bought nor sold any land is never recorded anywhere unless he committed some offence or was the subject of a plea. Some who appeared in court once or twice for disorderly conduct may usually have been well-behaved. Whether they were good or bad, there is no clue to what kinship, if any, these other Popes had with Simon and his wife and son.

THE BRIDGES

Thomas Bridge, the villager with the dairy herd, was one of the third generation of this family in the period 1310–1377 and together they cover the whole of it.

Agnes Bridge was the senior member, a widow with two sons, John and William: she and John gave up a half land to William, who handed it back to her for her life. As well as this land, she and John had a fishery between Manea and Coveney Bridge: they shared this with Maurice of the hythe and paid 7s. a year for it (September 1310). This, however, did not prevent her doing a little fishing in the lord's fishery for which she was presented in June 1324. The family must have lived at Downham Hythe for she and John and Maurice were responsible, with Nicholas of the hythe and Thomas of the hythe and also John Sinerles, for the upkeep of 'a certain causeway at Downham Hythe, which is called Coubrigs'. On one occasion they were all presented for neglecting the upkeep of the causeway. Maurice, a cottager, was amerced, and so was John Sinerles who had more than one river meadow, but both Nicholas and Thomas were 'pardoned because poor'. One gets the impression, throughout, that many of the hythe dwellers were very poor, picking up a precarious living by casual work. It is not known when Agnes died but it must have been before July 1328 for by then William's half land had reverted to him and he had sold it.

John Bridge was elected warden of the bylaw in July 1314. Like his father he married a woman named Agnes and they had a son, the Thomas of the dairy herd. John abandoned his half land: it was on the vacant lands list in May 1365. He died holding a river meadow, a house and one-third of the fishery between Manea and Coveney Bridge, all of which he left (26 April 1368) to Thomas. He must have died about February 1368 for on 2 March 1368 Thomas came to court and requested an inquest about putting boundaries between his holding and that of his mother, Agnes (not both parents). His request rather suggests some trouble about the inheritance. Three months later (July 1368) Thomas surrendered part of his river meadow (1½ roods) at Downham Hythe to Geoffrey Bridge and two years later he passed half an acre of alder grove to him: this suggests some relationship. After his father's death he seems to have been constantly in trouble and short of money: perhaps that was why he so soon sold part of his property. In May 1369 he 'did damage in and laid waste' his holding, and felled trees and sold them, and between that year and 1376 he was nine times in court for debt – no very large debts, the greatest was 40d. – but the frequency of his appearances suggests that it was very difficult to get money out of him, and there must have been many other debts settled out of court. He eventually sold the rest of his river meadow at Downham Hythe and his fishery called Dam in July 1376.

Geoffrey Bridge already had a river meadow when Thomas sold him the 1½ roods: the two meadows lay next to each other. Like Thomas, his interest lay in cattle and he had a bull: in April 1368 it did damage to the lord's meadow. As well as his meadows, Geoffrey had, in 1369/70, six acres of arable demesne land in 'le Botine' which he rented at 8d. an acre. Like some others, he abandoned his customary holding for free land: his full land appears as vacant in the list of March 1362. He was one of a group of rebels in 1375, refusing to scythe or reap in the harvest, for which he was amerced 12d. (the other three were fined only 3d. each) and neglecting to cut his 4000 turves for the lord, which cost him 6d. and a warning from the steward, with an order to do the work.

THE CARDINALS

Simon Cardinal was a customary tenant, a villager of some substance, appearing in the rolls from July 1311 to July 1331, when he died. He had two full lands and a half land: in December 1325 he gave the half land to a son, Geoffrey, who passed it back to him for the duration of his life; he gave one full land to another son, John, some time before July 1328 (when the unpaid heriot of 12s. was collected) and finally, when he died, he left the other full land to a third son, Hugo. As well as these customary holdings he rented a headland at 'Gradene-dene' for which he paid 4s. 4d. in the year 1318/19 and he sold a plot of land (28 square poles) to John Hayt in February 1329.

He had a flock of sheep. In September 1311 there is mention of his keeping in his fold ten sheep belonging to Nicholas the shepherd – sheep that should have been in the lord's fold. In July 1330 he was presented for having five sheep from Ely in his fold and also for crossing the lord's meadow with 30 sheep.

On 27 February 1316 he was elected reeve in the place of William Personn who had been dismissed, but he did not keep that office for long – the reeve's account for 1318/19 bears the name of Richard Kede. Simon was elected a custodian of the bylaw in July 1314 and custodian of the vill in July 1328. He was a juror in ten leets.

He and John Hayt were neighbours: in December 1327 he had allowed a drain between their lands to become stopped up and Hayt complained about this. They were certainly not good neighbours: before the trouble about the drain, in May 1327, Simon had made complaints (unspecified in the roll) against Hayt and his wife Juliana and his daughter Joanna. And in the same court he had falsely accused John Hayt of removing water from his pond, causing his fish to die. There seems to have been an old feud – back in 1315 (September) Simon had made a sad complaint – Hayt had trodden on him and he had claimed, and received, 6d. for damages.

Another case that Simon took to court was in December 1324, against the assessors of taxes for arms who, he said, had overcharged him for the tax on his holding. This time John Hayt was an ally – he and Robert the smith made similar accusations. But they were all unsuccessful in their pleas and were amerced 6d. each for 'making false clamour'.

Simon is mentioned in connection with several debts which suggests that he was occupied in trading in some commodity. In December 1313 an unspecified debt was due from him to the Master of the Hospital of St John of Ely, and 25s. was due to him from John of Wereham and his wife and Roger of Wysett and his wife, and an order for payment was made. In January 1326 Robert of the Green (chaplain) sued Simon for 35s. and a bushel of wheat. Minor debts included a quarter of barley worth 2s. due to the executors of Nicholas Scut (April 1328) and 4 bushels of corn which he owed to Nicholas de Caldecote (another chaplain) in December 1330.

Three times he owed wages to his servants: in September 1328, 14d. to Thomas atte hythe for reaping two acres of corn; in December 1330, Margaret de Coveney had not received her wages (8s.) for the previous year; on the same date Anota atte hythe complained that Simon, with Simon de Keten, had not paid her the sixpence 'which they paid her annually'.

He was presented a few times: in his early days (July 1311) for default of suit to the mill, for driving his cart through 'the middle enclosure of the fen' and for putting a mare and colt into the park without leave. These last two cost him fairly heavy amercements: twelve villagers were guilty of driving carts through the enclosure; they were all amerced 6d. while Simon had to pay a shilling. Two others had put mares and colts into the park; they had to pay 3d. each and he was charged 6d. In the harvests of 1325 and 1330 he failed to reap and carry corn at the proper time.

He married twice. In September 1329, less than two years before his death, he came to court, and asked the lord's leave to marry Matilda, the daughter of William Lovechild.

Simon Cardinal junior was a contemporary of Simon Cardinal, appearing in the roll as early as 1311. He can hardly have been his son, for the men who are known to have been Simon's sons are recorded only from 1325 (Geoffrey), 1328 (John) and 1331 (Hugo). He was perhaps a younger cousin of Simon Cardinal. He last appears in the roll in 1328.

His career was less colourful. There is no record of jurorship or of village office. He had some land next to that of Clement Brewster who asked (September 1311) that a boundary be placed between them, and an inquest on the matter was granted. Simon also had half an acre of land 'above Barleydonehone' which he exchanged with Simon Buk for half an acre 'in Parrok'.

His presentments were all in the year 1314: in September he had not done his harvest work for the lord, he had stolen eighteen sheaves of the lord's barley, carried rushes across the middle of the park and broken down the park fence. And in December he had 'drawn blood' from Robert the chaplain.

One debt is mentioned: Simon and five others (September 1312) were withholding from Agnes the wife of Adam the son of Philip the sum of 2s. 1½d. which the court considered should be paid at once.

Simon Cardinal's sons come next: first *Geoffrey*, who had the half land from his father (December 1325). Three months earlier he had been elected hayward 'by the whole homage', and he held that office until December 1328. He was reeve, with Simon Buk, in 1331/32 and then every year up to, at any rate, Michaelmas 1352 except for one year, 1347/48, when John Dumfrey took over from him. They shared that office in 1348/49 and after that Geoffrey resumed it, at any rate for three years. Because of the subsequent nine-year gap in the accounts it is not known how long he continued. He was elected hayward in September 1376.

A few debts suggest some trading: the executors of William Personn owed him 13s. (May 1330) and in the previous December he was ordered to pay '12s. of silver, due last Michaelmas' to one John, son of Lawrence of Ely. In both these matters he was in partnership with John Columbers. There is no indication of what the debts were for.

In July 1370 he took up, temporarily, 1½ acres of land, left vacant by the death of John Dumfrey, and the rent roll for that year (1370: Appendix I) shows that he was renting 2 acres in Holmhone and 4 in Stakehone, all at 8d. an acre.

He was juror in eleven courts between 1368 and 1376; he was constable of the watch (December 1373) and had the misfortune to be attacked by another villager, Stephen Frost.

He was presented twice: in December 1367 he did not turn up to do his 'works' and in March 1374, as a juror, he failed to present some damage done to Reginald Brewster's holding.

John Cardinal received his full land and messuage from his father before July 1328, when a 'heriot' of 12s. was found to have been unpaid and was collected.

Hugo Cardinal had his full land in July 1331 on his father's death. He was a juror in the leets of 1332, 1333 and 1334 and was elected a custodian of the bylaw in August 1334. On his marriage (November 1333) he refused to give a feast for the manor servants: this is delicately described in the roll as withdrawing 'from the said customary service'. One feels grateful to him for this information about such a custom.

There were six other Cardinals: *Reginald* was listed in the 1251 extent as a customary tenant with a full land and also four acres of assarted land at Apesholt. He may have been a grandfather of both the Simons mentioned above and perhaps also of *William* who was a juror in November 1310. *Stephen* died in 1346/47 and his heriot was a stot worth 5s. and *Ralph* held a quarter land which appeared on the vacant list in June 1373.

Katerina kept sheep: 40 were in the lord's pasture (December 1362). The following year, in September, 8 of her piglets were at pannage in the park. She had a three-quarter land, and in May 1368 she took up a river meadow lying next to John Hayt's. In March 1365 she was granted leave to have an inquest on her boundary with Roger Brewster. On one occasion (April 1366) she did not come to work when summoned. In September 1373 her three-quarter land was on the vacant list.

And there was another *Geoffrey Cardinal,* a cottager who was presented in May 1369 for having 40 sheep outside the lord's fold. He came on hard times and from November 1375 to July 1377 was regularly before the court, being ordered to produce pledges for the repair of his dilapidated holding.

THE KEDES

There were eight villagers with this surname. The earliest was *Ralph Kede,* with half a full land in 1251. Some or all of the others may have descended from him, but no relationships among them can be proved.

Richard Kede belongs to the earlier period of the rolls. He was a customary tenant, with a full land, a cotland and a fishery: the fishery he sold to Geoffrey Scut in July 1331 and the cotland he sold, or gave, to Agnes the daughter of Thomas March in May 1325. He may already have had some link with that family: ten years later his daughter Agnes married William de March.

In October 1322 he bought six acres of land from Richard Eliot and made with him the arrangement whereby Eliot was to keep two acres of the land for the duration of his life and make to Kede annual payments of sedges and turves and all the dung from his two acres. The following year he sold two acres of land to a freeman, Simon de Ketene.

Richard was a juror in every court of the earlier series, reeve for two years from Michaelmas 1318 and was five times elected custodian of the bylaw. He was also an assessor of taxes for arms, in which capacity he was falsely accused by three villagers for overcharging them.

He was presented a few times: twice for failing to do harvest work and once for receiving stolen corn from the warrener. He was sued four times, three of these debts he owed to William Shepherd with whom he seems to have done some business, for he owed him, besides 6½ quarters of malting barley, '8s. for ploughs, carts, etc.' that Shepherd had sold to him, and payment for the keep of one of Richard's oxen for two years.

He may well have been one of the victims of the Black Death for it is the reeve's account of 1350/51 that tells of his death: he died without heirs and his remaining chattels went to the lord: '2 cows, 2 bullocks, 1 piglet and 680 rushes in place of 13s. he owed to the lord for rushes'. His full land and half land appear in the lists of vacant lands in 1362 and 1366.

Reginald Kede, who acquired a full land and a half land by his marriage to the widow of Simon Pope in July 1328, was a juror in December 1328 and at the next six leets. He bought an acre of land from a freeman in 1329. His two presentments concerned harvest work and trespass with six geese: he had three debts, none larger than seven bushels of malting barley. His full land and his half land appear as vacant in the lists of 1362 and 1373.

Simon Kede also belongs to the earlier period. He had a half land and a cotland and was twice (1316 and 1330) elected hayward. He let an acre of land to Nicholas Scut in February 1327 for four harvests. Two of his offences, also, concerned harvest work: two others were regarded as serious and he was amerced 6d. for each of them – he broke down the park fence in his early days and in July 1328 he 'refused to bring John the miller to Somersham, which all tenants must do for 5d.' One wonders why he refused such a remunerative job! In March 1362 he was reported to have 'died some time ago' and his half land and cotland went to his widow Caterina and her new husband, Simon Rote.

Adam Kede was active in the 1360s and 1370s. His status is unrecorded but he must have had some customary land, for he had his beasts impounded in November 1368 for not fulfilling his services and dues. He 'broke the pound' and retrieved them, for which he was presented. In spite of this truculent behaviour he seems to have been regarded as a responsible member of the vill: he was juror at every court but four in the latter series and was at various times ale-taster, custodian of the bylaw, coroner of stock and custodian of the fen and it was he who, when acting as constable of the watch, was attacked by Stephen Frost. He appears in the 1369/70 rent roll as holding, at 8d. an acre, 2½ acres in Stakehone, a rood in 'le Botine', 2 roods in le Heath and an acre in Acreland. He seems to have had a quarrel with another villager, Hugo Prest: he killed one of Hugo's piglets (damage 2s.) and they damaged each other's crops. He had a daughter, Katerina, who married the son of John Cok.

The other two Kedes are *John Richard,* who owed a small debt in 1312, and *another Simon,* of the later series, who was one of the unfortunates with dilapidated holdings constantly before the court in the closing years of the period.

THE LOVECHILDS

Philip Lovechild was a cottager. In December 1325 he was presented for having 'fifteen sheep and lambs in Simon Pope's fold and not where every cottager should have his sheep'. In February 1327 he rented 5 roods of land from Hugo

Shepherd for three harvests and 3½ acres from John Man for five harvests. He had a wife, Agnes, and a son, William. He died in, or shortly before, December 1329.

In December 1326 *William* acquired a half land and a house from William Dumfrey and his wife Amicia. Three years later, after his father had died, his mother *Agnes* came to court and claimed William's half land as her dower, saying that Philip, her husband, had owned it before their marriage. An inquest found that it was as Agnes had said, that 'Philip had acquired the land for himself and Agnes his wife for their whole lives and for William their son after their deaths'. William disputed this and fortunately had the sense to ask that a scrutiny be made of the roll of December 1326 and the scrutiny of course proved the land to be his by right.

Agnes had other land: she sold six acres of assarted land at Apesholt in February 1333. And she made another false claim, this time in September 1333, against John Man for one quarter and seven bushels of corn.

William was at one time a custodian of the 'New Ditch'. Twice he was in slight trouble, once for driving his cart over a neighbour's corn (October 1324) and once for failing to reap the lord's barley at the proper time (September 1330). He had two daughters, both of whom appear in the roll in September 1329 as prospective brides, *Agnes* to marry Robert Eliot and *Matilda* to marry Simon Cardinal. William died in or before the year 1347/48, when a 'heriot' of one ox was paid, which suggests that he had acquired a further half land, for the 'heriot' for a half land was only half a beast (July 1328). Anyway he, unlike his father, was a customary tenant.

John Lovechild, of the later period, was a customary tenant, twice elected reeve (September 1364 and September 1376), and a juror in 37 of the 49 courts of the later years. From 1374 to 1377 he was constantly standing pledge for unfortunate villagers who had been ordered to repair their dilapidated houses. He was elected custodian of the fen in 1362, ale-taster in 1368, custodian of the bylaw in 1370 and attendant of stock in March 1376. The rent roll of 1369/70 shows that, like Adam Kede, he rented 2½ acres of demesne at 8d. an acre in Stakehone, and the court roll (December 1373) that he rented 1¾ acres 'over Holmhone' for one year, for corn. He had a daughter, *Joanna*, who married Robert Rote in 1366: nothing is recorded of his wife or of any other children. It is strange to read, about this seemingly responsible member of the community, that in July 1376 he was presented, with two others, for 'laying waste the fen', and for this he had to pay the heavy amercement of 40d. His only other recorded offence was that of letting twelve sheep damage the lord's crops in May 1369.

There were two more Lovechilds, Geoffrey and Henry. *Geoffrey* snared a woodcock 'to the spoiling of the warren of the lord' (December 1328). Of *Henry* is recorded his 'heriot', 'an ox or part of an ox' in the reeve's account for 1348/49, so he was a customary tenant with a full land or a half land.

THE SAUSERS

Of the *Sausers* there were: one family of five, two married couples, and one man. To take the family first:

John Sauser was a customary tenant holding a full land. He was juror in the leets of 1310, 1311 and 1315, and warden of the bylaw (July 1311 and July 1314). He had a wife *Katerina*, a son *John* and a daughter *Agnes*. It was to Katerina that he left his full land and when she died it passed (April 1328) not to her son but to her grandson *Richard Sauser*. Maybe her son John had died. The most colourful incident about this family is recorded in December 1313 when John senior was presented for 'harbouring Robert the park-keeper and other strangers not of good repute'. His son John had 'gone out at night with the said Robert, knowing him to be of ill-repute'. John senior's other indiscretions were not so exciting – he cut fodder on the common land before St John the Baptist's Day, 24 June (July 1311) and he cut grass on the baulks between the lord's strips of barley. Of Agnes it is recorded that in December 1325 'leyrwite' had to be paid, and for once the roll gives the name of the 'other party', William of Holkham.

The two couples were Robert and Joanna, Henry and Alice. *Robert*, son of William (William does not appear elsewhere), the lessee of a fishery 'from Robert Morris' dam to Sidditch' married *Joanna*, a daughter of William of Stoneye. In June 1315 they bought half a rood of land from a widow, Isabella Stot and in December that year they both renounced all right and claim to a small piece of land (28 square poles) which Joanna's father was selling to Robert Hastler. There is nothing to help with the status of Robert Sauser. He appears once in the record of offences: he 'struck and tore the flesh' of William the reeve, causing damage to the extent of 6d. (May 1314). *Henry Sauser* held a quarter land as well as a cotland, so was a customary tenant. He had bought the quarter land from Geoffrey Morris. When he died (November 1334) he left both lands to his widow *Alice* to hold for her life: the heriot was 'a fourth part of horse, worth 6s.' Nichols Scut's executors sued him for the sum of 3s. 6d. for six bushels of barley.

Simon Sauser, also, was a customary tenant: in May 1325 he bought from Agnes Buk a half land which had just come to her on the death of her father, Robert Buk. Simon was hayward for one year from December 1329. He was a juror in the leets from 1325 to 1330 and from 1332 to 1334 and was elected warden of the fen in April 1326. With William Lovechild he committed two offences: he drove his cart over a neighbour's corn (October 1324) and failed to reap the lord's corn (September 1325). He was concerned in two debts: in October 1322 he had lent 8d. to John Man who was too poor to repay it and the court excused him, and in December 1325 Simon had borrowed 40d. from Richard the wright and was ordered to repay it.

THE SINERLES

John Sinerles is never mentioned in connection with land in the open fields and it is not known whether he had a full land, a cotland or no land in the fields at all. Nor is he mentioned in connection with sheep, so there is no help there with his status. He almost certainly lived away from the main village, down at Downham Hythe, for he acquired, around there, his river meadows, fisheries and pieces of land. Perhaps he had some employment or picked up bits of work in connection with the waterway. He certainly had some stock and a need for some land and in July 1314 he was granted a river meadow and half an acre in the common fen at Downham Hythe to hold by services and a shilling a year: this payment appears in every account up to 1374/75. In 1315 he bought from his brother *Reginald* another river meadow, and also a rood of land which he passed to *Henry Sinerles* (perhaps a son, but no relationship is stated) fourteen years later. In 1369/70 he rented one of the demesne acres of land being let at 8d. in 'the cultura next to Downham Hythe' and 3¼ acres at 8d. in 'le Botine' (Appendix I). Entries in the reeve's accounts for 1345/46 to 1374/75 show that he had the forethought to rent for a penny a year a perch of land on which to deposit dung. He was also something of a fisherman: he acquired one fishery (stretching from that of Robert Allen to Downham Hythe) in June 1324, another (from Downham Hythe to the Park) in 1330/31 – and he held this one for twenty years. In 1374/75 he rented the Manea fishery for 3s. a year. In 1328 he was elected a custodian of the new ditch and in March 1362 a custodian of the fen and he was a juror in sixteen courts between 1362 and 1370. His only recorded offence was in the early years – if, in fact, it was he and not an earlier John: in November 1311 he had neglected to repair the causeway at Downham Hythe and was amerced 3d. There is no indication that any of the other Sinerles, except his brother Reginald, were kin to him.

There was a *Richard Sinerles* with a wife *Margaret* in the later series of rolls: she rented 1¾ acres of demesne near Downham Hythe in 1369/70. They had a son John who bought from Thomas Bridge in July 1376 a river meadow, a fishery called Daam and half a rood of land at Downham Hythe.

There was also a *Robert* of no particular interest; also, in the later years, a *Simon Sinerles* whose half land and quarter land are on the vacant lands list in May 1365: and (perhaps another) *Simon,* who is a juror seven times between 1364 and 1368 and appears, like John, on the 1369/70 rent roll as holding an acre 'in the cultura next to Downham Hythe' for 8d. and who, in the year 1373/74, rented two acres of demesne land 'over Crouchone' at 1s. an acre for growing corn.

THE STONEYES

Near the village of Downham, eight miles to the north west, is the little hamlet of Stoneye (Stonea) and there are constant references to people with that surname. There are records of eleven of them: some were certainly related to each other but whether the rest were kin to them or were named 'of Stoneye' because they came from there is not known.

Simon of Stoneye comes first: both the extents show that he held a full land in Downham.

William of Stoneye appears in the records from 1311 to 1332. At first he was a cottager (presented in September 1311 for keeping sheep outside the lord's fold) renting from Simon Allen 10 acres of villein land, for the duration of his life. In July 1328, however, he claimed (and in December proved by scrutiny of the roll) his right to a full land surrendered by Etheldreda daughter of John Dolre. No indication is given as to why he had this right and the relative roll must be one of those that are missing. While he was still a cottager he made two transactions: he bought a fishery at Sidditch from Juliana the gardener in June 1315 and in December of that year he sold to Robert Hasteler three-quarters of a rood from his messuage. Later, in May 1329, an inquest showed that he had bought half an acre of free land from a freeman.

He had a wife, *Amicia,* a son Robert and two daughters, *Rose* who married (May 1314) Roger Rede of Chettisham and another who married (January 1331) Adam Buk who had a little difficulty in getting from William the twelve marks due to be paid on the marriage.

In March 1332 it was found that William had handed 'his lands' (that is, his full land) to his son Robert without leave and he was presented for this and amerced 3d. Soon after this he must have died, for by 25 September 1333 Amicia had re-married. She appeared in court on that day requesting 'an inquest and a jury to decide the endowing of the said Amicia with the land which belonged to William her former husband, according to the custom of the manor'. The result of the inquest is not recorded then or later, but a later reference (31 August 1334) to a failure by Robert to supply corn to his mother shows that he was holding the land and giving her maintenance. At Amicia's death (recorded on 8 February 1335) she was holding 7¾ acres of free demesne land for which she was paying eightpence an acre: this land went to her new husband Nicholas Allen. Amicia and her son Robert, it seems, were not on the best of terms with each other. She had to sue him for one payment of corn and in the previous court he was presented for making some false accusation against her. Some years earlier (December 1330) he 'drew blood' from her and she raised a hue and cry on him.

But to return to William: he was a juror at ten recorded leets between 1311 and 1332 and was elected a coroner of stock in April 1336. He was reeve from Michaelmas 1321 for four years, possibly five years — the account for 1325/26 is missing. As a reeve he was sometimes a little lax in making payments for work: John Hayt had to sue him for 15d. for thirty 'works' and Simon Cardinal had not been paid 12d. wages due to him and two bushels of corn as allowances. He had a few private debts also: he did some threshing for Clement the brewer and did not return nine bushels of dredge to him and also owed him for half a bushel of malt. He owed William of Hotham two quarters of malt barley worth 13s. 4d. He was sued by the miller in September 1325 and had to pay his debts, but in May 1327 when the miller sued him again for 29s. 4½d. William waged his law three-handed and won his case. He seems to have done some trading with Simon Pope whom he sued for an unstated amount in 1324, but eventually they came to an agreement. After Pope's death William was suing his executors and obtained payments of eight shillings and 1½ quarters of corn worth five shillings.

He was presented a few times, twice on matters that were regarded as serious and for each of which he was amerced 12d.: he cut fodder on the common before St John the Baptist's Day (24 June) and he cut sixty bundles of the lord's osiers. Otherwise, eight of his geese damaged the lord's rye; twice he neglected his drains; twice he ploughed where he should not (30 perches x 1 foot in the road by the hythe and 5 perches x 1 foot in Cardinal's Lane) and once, unwisely, he dug a ditch (6 perches x 1 foot) against the gate of the manor: this ditch cost him 6d.

Amicia seems to have been an aggressive member of the community. When Hugo de Kendal impounded her goose causing her some loss (he had to pay 8d. damages) she retaliated by going for him, causing damage assessed at 10d. And when Amicia Bronn was unwise enough to slander her (damages 3d.) she beat Amicia and 'drew blood' from Isabel Bronn, her daughter, and all that cost her 9d.

In September 1332 *Robert Stoneye,* in possession of the full land from his father, bought a messuage from the chaplain, Robert son of Richard le Keu. Le Keu was to hold it for life and pay Stoneye six marks a year. He must have died very soon afterwards for on 3 February 1333 Stoneye sold the messuage to Walter of Stretham and Agnes his wife.

Robert married Rosa, daughter of Geoffrey Smith who had much difficulty in finding the money, five marks and eight shillings, due to be paid on the marriage. At the same time Geoffrey owed Robert three marks for a blanket (this suggests trading by Robert) and the two men came to an agreement that payment should be made in seven instalments of one mark and one, the last, of 21s. 4d., on stated dates between Lent 1328 and St John the Baptist's Day 1329.

Robert seems to have been a quarrelsome man. All his appearances in court concern, not offences against the lord, but wrongs done to other villagers or disputes with them. He broke an agreement with Robert Hasteler about a certain half acre of peas (September 1330), wrongly raised a hue against him (December 1330) and had to be sued by him for a bushel of corn worth 8d. (January 1331). He took John le Sherman's harrow (March 1331) and had to pay damages 12d. He poached in Simon Warin's fishery and then (Simon presumably objecting) he beat him (July 1331). The one entry (November 1333) which concerns the 'establishment' is revealing and tells of a customary service which must have been an unwelcome burden to some villagers. It reads: 'also they [the jurors] say that every villein who has taken a wife must feed the servants of the manor according to custom. Hugo Cardinal (3d.), Robert de Stoneye (3d.), John Child (3d.) and John Wareyn (3d.) withdrew from the said customary service. Therefore they are in mercy. And an order was made to raise the money, etc.' So, when Robert had married Rosa about four years earlier he had not feasted the manor servants and was now to pay an equivalent sum to the lord.

There is only one more Stoneye belonging to the earlier years, *Anota*, twice in court for slander and defamation of character. All the others are found in the later series of rolls, and there is no hint of kin to each other or to the earlier Stoneyes. *Katerina* can be quickly disposed of: John Kendall 'drew her blood'. The remaining three are: Geoffrey, John and Rosa.

The first record of *Geoffrey* is on 16 March 1362 (the earliest court of the later series) when his name appears on the list of vacant lands: his half land was taken up by Stephen Frost. He had secured other land for which he paid rent. He appears on the rent roll of 1369/70, but only as holding 4½ acres in le Botine and in Acreland at 8d. an acre. There is no guide to his status after 16 March 1362. He must have been regarded as a reliable member of the community for he was juror at sixty of the sixty-one courts of the later series, elected a coroner of stock once and a custodian of the bylaw once. He was presented three times: for failing to keep watch, for breaking suit of mill and (September 1373) for carrying off the crop from Simon Rote's half acre. Damages amounted to two bushels of corn (presumably the half acre crop) and '6d. for ploughing'.

John Stoneye's story is much the same: his half land was on the vacant lands list in May 1365: after he parted with it he was no longer a customary tenant and was presented (May 1369) for keeping twenty sheep outside the lord's fold. Like Geoffrey he was frequently a juror (thirty-four times between 1364 and 1370) and, like Geoffrey, he broke suit of mill, grinding 4 bushels elsewhere. He was once presented for bad harvesting and once for breaking Alan Draper's fish-trap and then beating him: the damages were 9d.

Rosa Stoneye rented an acre in Acreland for 8d. in the year 1369/70. Her daughter Isabel married John, son of Ralph (March 1365). She was once presen-

(5) One of the two remaining portions of the fifteenth century palace, now part

ted for failing to do her 'works'. She was eventually one of those whose dilapidated holdings occupied much of the court's attention from 1374 to 1376: her cottage finally became a ruin.

Individual Villagers

Stephen Frost is of interest not only for his aggressive habits (his fights, his attack on the constables and his breaking of arrest) but also because he rented a bakehouse and this is the only reference in the rolls to such a place. In May 1365 he took over from Robert Rote a half land, a cotland and the bakehouse, to rent for six years at 40d. a year. In the course of these six years, in November 1368, another interesting entry appeared in the roll: Stephen was presented for 'stealing bread twice'. This suggests that he not only baked the bread that he had made himself, but that some villagers who had made their bread at home brought the loaves to him for baking and that on two occasions he returned fewer loaves than he had received.

The accounts show that in 1367/68 and in 1368/69 Frost rented an acre of demesne land at 1s. an acre: neither the field nor the cultura is indicated. The rent roll of 1369/70, however, shows that in that year he had an acre at 1s. in the cultura called Churchill and two acres at 8d. in Holmhone. The court roll shows, in July 1374, that for ten years from Michaelmas 1374 he was to rent two acres in Churchill (called Chyrchone here) at 1s. and two acres in Shepehone at 8d., payments to be made in equal portions at the usual four seasons. (The accounts for 1374/75 vaguely enter only 1s. for this rent that year; this was probably copied from earlier accounts!)

William Hayt was one of those who, in the bad later years, abandoned a holding – his cotland appears in the 'vacant' list of May 1365 but he was still in the vill after that date. He must, however, have held a full land or half land as well, for he was presented in April 1368 for damage by 30 sheep, not for keeping sheep outside the lord's fold. In July of that year he received from his father John a river meadow 'just as it lay between William Shepherd's river meadow and that of Katerina Cardinal': the rent was a penny a year. In September 1369 he was elected by the homage to take up a vacant half land and that same year (1369/70) he was also renting 10¾ acres of demesne at 8d. an acre. In 1373/74 he rented a further 2 acres for one year, 'for corn', at 1s. an acre.

He was a juror in 38 of the 49 courts of the later series and was elected custodian of the fen, three times custodian of the bylaw, twice an ale-taster, and twice some sort of reeve (not the reeve of the accounts: that office was held by John Wrong).

William was once guilty of default of suit of mill and one debt (5s.) is recorded.

Thomas Holt is not mentioned in connection with any customary holding or any office. He is of interest for his industry in renting demesne land and fisheries. In 1361/62 he paid rent for 2 acres at 1s. 4d. an acre (and a 'gersuma' of 1s.). In October 1367 he took up 6 acres of demesne to hold for ten years at 1s. an acre, and he paid 4d. for 'time', for the privilege of renting for a definite term of years. The rent roll of 1369/70 shows that in that year he was holding a total of 12½ acres:

> 2 acres at 1s. 4d. 'in the cultura between the mill and Redefinere'.
> 1½ acres at 8d. in Holmhone.
> 9 acres at 8d. in Stakehone.

And he was renting fisheries just as busily:

> The Newditch and Parkditch for two years in December 1362 (rents not shown).
> The Newditch (4d. a year), Park Ditch (2s.), Downham Hythe (6d.) in 1367/68 and 1368/69.

He bought a house in March 1362 from Isabella Bannesquynne.

John Man is most remarkable for his debts. He was sued four times in 1311, once in 1312, twice in 1314 and once in 1322, 1328 and 1329. The debts in 1311 were all for sedges – 1300, 500 and (twice) 1000. Once in 1314 he owed 500 turves. Three times his debts were of money (8d., 3d. and ½d) and once he owed for 'a chest worth 1s.' On one occasion he was not amerced, he was 'pardoned because poor'.

In February 1327, finding it more profitable than tilling his land, he sublet 5 acres of it to three villagers for three or five harvests, sold half an acre to another and in 1329 sold a small plot (6 square poles) to his brother Richard and his family.

His other appearances in court concerned bad harvest work and harbouring strangers in his younger days and (later, 1326–1328) stealing 12 sheaves of corn, failing to clear a ditch 'and thereby ruining the fishing for the time being' and poaching fish in the lord's ditch. Nevertheless he was elected custodian of the new ditch in 1328, (a dyke-reeve under the commission for sewers).

William Personn comes into the picture as a cottager, presented in September 1311 for having ten sheep outside the lord's fold. However, in December 1314 he bought, from his man, Richard Kebbe, the half land and messuage, the cotland and two acres which were later, on Kebbe's death (26 June 1324) the subject of a claim for dower by Kebbe's widow, but this claim was unsuccessful and William retained the lands. Also, at some time he came by a full land, and when he died (11 September 1329) he left it and the other land to his widow *Juliana.* When she died (September 1332) she left all the lands to *Simon her son* and at the next court (December 1332) he sold the half land and the cotland to his brother *Henry* — who then let them to Simon for ten years. Thus it was that Henry was in possession of the half land and cotland when, in June 1333, Kebbe's widow renewed her claim to dower, this time successfully; but she did not get the lot, as she had claimed originally; she got one-third of the cotland and half the half land. So Henry was left with half a half land and two-thirds of a cotland and Simon still held the full land.

Simon, like his father, had had some dealings with Nicholas Scut whose executors owed him 1½ quarters of barley worth 5s. He once neglected work at harvest, and was once a juror (November 1333). He married Joanna the daughter of John Columbers. He died in the year 1346/47 and the heriot due was an ox.

As well as the two sons there was a *daughter, Agnes Personn,* to whom Reginald Kede owed, in December 1331, 7 bushels of malting barley. In the early years, 1311, there was a *John Personn,* possibly William's brother, who bought a house from Richard the fletcher, and a plot of land from Simon Pope and paid rent to the lord for these — a penny a year for the house and a half-penny a year for the land.

To return to *William*: he was a juror at seven leets and affeerer in six courts between 1311 and 1328, was elected warden of the bylaw in July 1311 and again in September 1325, a warden of the fen in April 1326, a keeper of the warren in February 1328 and a custodian of the vill in July 1328. He was an ale-taster for some period up to December 1313 and again for some period up to his death.

He was presented for various misdeeds: in July 1311 (with other villagers) for driving his cart across an enclosure in the fen; in September 1312 for allowing his servant to cut the grass on the baulks between the lord's strips of barley; in December 1315 for himself cutting 60 bundles of osiers in the lord's osier bed; in October 1322 for neglect of harvest work. But it was on 27 February 1316 that he was really in trouble. He was reeve at the time and the jurors reported that:

1. He had used one of the lord's oxen for two days to cart his own sedges in the fen; and he had used one of the lord's horses for one day to cart his own timber from Ely to his home, and the horse had had no rest between whiles.
2. He had taken 5s. worth of the lord's timber and had used one of the lord's carts to carry it to his own home.
3. He had used one of the lord's carts to carry a cartload of his own sedges to Stretham.
4. And he had used one to take two cart-loads of his own turves to Ely.
5. And one to cart his own peas from the field Aggrave.
6. He had used one of the lord's servants for three days, stacking his corn.
7. He had committed adultery with the wife of Robert Morris and
8. He had allowed her to take away from the manor hay and forage worth 4d.

9.   His servant, John Paste, had taken a post from the manor: it was worth 1d.
10. He had not supervised visiting carters and they had taken sheaves of oats and 2 quarters of fodder from the barn.
11. He had slaughtered three pigs at his own meat store [some of this membrane is illegible here and the charge is not understood].
12. He had overcharged for sheaves that he had taken for fodder for the horses from Lammastide to All Saints' Day by a quarter and half a bushel.
13. With Simon Pope he had collected a fine from a negligent swineherd (three pigs had died through the man's neglect) and he had kept more of his share of the fine by 2s.
14. He had allowed the lord's plough-teams to lie idle from time to time, 'in summer and in autumn for three weeks'. [The steward accepted William's excuse for this: it was 'because of stormy weather and poor kitchen transport'.]

William was ordered to pay damages amounting to 25s. 10d. to the lord and 2s. to Simon Pope and an amercement of 10s. and he was dismissed. Simon Cardinal was elected by the whole homage, as reeve in his place.

His debts, which were fairly large, suggest considerable trading or they may have been due from the demesne and therefore his responsibility.

33s. 6d. to Ralph Valentine (September 1325) for 4 quarters of malt which he undertook to pay by Martinmas.

20s. to John the fisherman (December 1326) for corn, to be paid at midsummer (St John the Baptist's Day) and Michaelmas.

An unspecified debt to Walter the brewster of Ely (December 1326).

5s. and 2 quarters of barley which he had agreed to pay to Nicholas Scut, who died, and the debt was collected by his executors (April 1328). This would be paid at Michaelmas.

1 quarter of barley worth 4s., to Nicholas Scut, also collected by his executors (April 1328).

10s. to Henry le Fenland (December 1329): to be paid by William's executors, half at Christmas and half on St John the Baptist's Day.

13s. to John de Columbers and Geoffrey Cardinal, trading in partnership (May 1330) to be paid by William's executors.

It was reported by a jury of inquest in court on 27 June 1329 that William's house had been burned down and the holding which had been worth 4s. was now worth only 12d. He was ordered to rebuild the house. This is the only reference in these papers to the loss of a house by fire. Three months later (11 September 1329) his death is recorded. His executors were his widow and Robert the smith and the 'heriot' paid was a horse worth 10s.

Hugo Shepherd acquired a half land by marrying Amicia the widow of Adam of the hythe in June 1315. Adam, however, had on his death left another half land and a house to Isabella, the daughter of himself and Amicia, and in February 1333 Isabella handed over this half land and house to her mother Amicia and her stepfather Hugo. They agreed 'separately' to pay her every year, as rent, at Michaelmas 6 bushels of wheat and at the Feast of the Purificiation half a quarter of barley and two bushels of peas and beans. If the payment should fall into arrears Isabella would have the right to take possession again of the land and house.

Like John Man, Hugo sublet some of his land for three years without leave. Four others had done this on a smaller scale, subletting an acre or less, and on 12 February 1327 they were all rounded up in court and amerced a penny for every sublet. Hugo had let a total of 5½ acres to five villagers. All the lessees were allowed to continue the arrangements on payment of a fine. The fines were 3d. or 6d. on every transaction: the amount bore no relation to the acreage.

Geoffrey the smith held a quarter land (the land in respect of which Geoffrey Morris falsely accused him in June 1335 in a plea of land)[2] and acquired other lands – half an acre from John Man (February 1327), two acres from 'a free-man' (May 1329) and an acre and a half of 'free land from a freeman' (July 1331). He also, in February 1327, rented from Hugo Shepherd an acre and a half for three harvests. All these transactions were made without leave and this was subsequently adjusted. He also, for seven years, rented a house from Emma Souter and this transaction was the cause of another false accusation against Smith, Emma's plea of covenant of 30 June 1335.[3]

He had a son, John, his 'first born and heir' and two daughters, Matilda, who married in October 1322 (her husband's name is not given) and Rosa who married Robert Stoneye (February 1327). On the occasion of the latter marriage he had some difficulty in paying the agreed dowry '5 marks and 8s.' He owed Robert, also, for a blanket worth 3 marks and on 24 February 1328 he agreed in court to pay off both debts by midsummer 1329, in eight instalments. He was to pay for the blanket first, a mark at mid-Lent, a mark at Easter and the final mark at Pentecost 1328. Then, for the dowry, similar payments at the Feasts of the Nativity of St John the Baptist (24 June), the Exaltation of the Holy Cross (14 September), and the Purification (2 February); and the final instalment of 21s. 4d. on St John the Baptist's Day 1329.

His misdemeanours were varied: he cut fodder in the common fen before St John the Baptist's Day in 1311 and he destroyed some trees on villein land (December 1322). Both these offences were serious and cost him 6d. each. He made an embankment by the Church Ditch in Simon Keten's land (December

2 See Chapter III.
3 See Chapter VIII: Pleas of covenant.

1325); once he reaped the lord's corn badly and once would not reap at all. In December 1322 he was a troublesome neighbour to Emma Pope; as well as damaging her wall he harassed her and was ordered 'to remain peacefully in his home under pain of loss'.

His son, *John Smith*, held the half land that he obtained from the Scut family after it had passed through the hands of the three Scut brothers. He agreed (September 1329) to pay Philip Scut two quarters of wheat, two quarters of barley and half a quarter of beans and peas in equal portions at the Feasts of the Annunciation, the Nativity of St John the Baptist, St Michael and St Andrew, for the duration of Philip's life.

CONCLUSION

This study of Downham-in-the-Isle was made in order to learn something of the various aspects of the village life in the thirteenth and fourteenth centuries and also to find out what changes took place during that time and the reasons for those changes.

Downham was a fair-sized nucleated village. It owed much of its importance to the fact that the Bishop of Ely, the lord of the manor, had a palace there and cultivated his demesne. The arable part of the demesne lay, with the holdings of the tenants, in three open fields beside the village. All the normal crops of corn and legumes were grown by the lord and the villagers and they compared well with those grown by other ecclesiastical manors.

The vill was a highly organized community. It was divided into groups (tithings) with mutual responsibility for behaviour: the chiefs of the tithings were also jurors in the court. They were men of some standing among the villeins and performed the administrative duties of the vill under the auspices of the manorial court which was held, normally, four times a year.

The holdings of the villagers were, officially, in two standard sizes, the full land of fourteen acres (often divided into half lands) and the cotland of one acre. In return for these customary lands the tenants rendered customary dues and specified 'works' for the lord, mostly on the demesne, but also in the Ely Palace or on public works such as dykes and the Aldreth causeway. Some villeins increased their acres by assarting land in the fen or renting acres of demesne land; for these they paid money-rent and did not render services.

For many, however, the main source of livelihood was not the holding, but the sheep: this was a sheep-farming village. Nearly every villager had some sheep; some of the tenants, even some of the cottagers, had considerably flocks — for with free pasture in the fen the size of a holding was of little importance. The sheep, and there must have been hundreds of them, were of course valuable for their manure but much greater profit was derived from their famous wool — and the wool trade was booming.

The fen was all-important to the village: besides the lush pasture for stock in the drier parts it provided fish and fowl, peat for fuel and building, sedge for building and thatch. All this, like the open-field farming, was organized — there was a law of the common fen.

Up to 1258 the drainage of the fens was a matter of local responsibility, a matter of 'ancient custom', but that year saw the first of a series of commissions for sewers (drains) and in time the commission undertook the supervision of all fen drainage, causing new dykes to be made and appointing officers in charge of their maintenance.

Transport to and from the village was by land or water, by land to Ely whence came 'the king's high road' that passed the length of the village and out to the west to Downham Hythe two miles away. The road would be much used by carts, some with considerable loads, and must have been well enough constructed to bear such traffic. A navigable waterway connected Downham Hythe with much of the fenland.

Until the early years of the fourteenth century Downham was a prosperous community: the population was growing, fresh assarts were being taken in from the fen, agriculture and sheep-farming were flourishing. This state of affairs may have continued until about 1319 — there is no evidence (owing to lack of records) that the manor suffered in 1315 and 1316 from the drenching summers and disastrous harvests that occurred in most parts of England. Downham's earliest known disaster was the unidentified epidemic amongst the animals known as the 'murrain' which visited the place in 1319/20. The reeve's account for that year records the deaths from murrain of 16 oxen, 4 cows and 18 bullocks and heifers and the land under cultivation by the demesne decreased that year by forty acres on account of the shortage of draught animals.

The villagers' losses must have been quite as serious as those of the lord and it is surprising, therefore, to find that by 1321/22 they had taken up 187 acres of demesne land newly released by him, thus increasing their demesne acreage to 348. There must have been a few draught animals left in the village and no doubt these would be lent and borrowed — and worked very hard indeed. Moreover, this well-tilled, convenient demesne land was a bargain at a shilling an acre; and the tenants now had more time, for the lord (with his sown acreage reduced to 112) no longer required all their customary services. They owed 3700 'works' a year: they were now, and for the next five years, to commute half of these and all their ploughing dues (133⅓ acres a year) at a penny or a halfpenny a 'work' and at threepence an acre. (Table XX)

The economy was again upset in 1327/28. In that year dire calamity fell: some virulent epidemic attacked Downham and fourteen customary tenants died — fourteen out of a total of, perhaps, thirty holders of full lands and half lands, half the chief men of the village. Their deaths are traceable in connection with the transfer of their lands and the payments of heriot: the deaths of other members of their families and of other villagers are not revealed by the records so their numbers can only be guessed: one might hazard a guess that the place must have lost quite half of its population. This serious depopulation caused another change in the pattern of the farming of the demesne: the lord was obliged to take back into his own cultivation over ninety acres because there were no tenants for them. The demesne rents dropped 33⅓%, from 1s., 1s. 6d., 2s. and 2s. 6d to 8d., 1s., 1s. 4d and 1s. 8d. For about ten years after the epidemic the lord, with more land and short of labour, again required the customary ploughing and the other works and practically no commuting was allowed.

In spite of the high mortality amongst the villagers (and a recurrence of murrain in 1328/29) no vacant customary lands are recorded at this time: a fresh tenant was found for every holding vacated by the death of an owner.

During the second decade after the epidemic the population was gradually recovering, the tenants were farming more of the demesne and were again commuting some of their works (about three-quarters of them) and all of their ploughing dues. It was not until 1346, however, that things were again stable; the acreage farmed by the tenants had by then reached 276. The rents then, inevitably, went up: they were increased by 50%, to their former level. It had taken nearly twenty years for the village to recover from the consequences of the disastrous epidemic.

There was little time for the recovery to be enjoyed, however, before the Black Death descended on the village. The death roll was great, but not so great as that of 1327/28. This time heriot payments were recorded for seven full-land holders and two half-landers – nine customary tenants out of about thirty – so one might hazard a guess that about one-third of the population died. The reeve's account for 1348/49 contains this sad note: 'No turves made this year for lack of men and mortality of men through the great pestilence'. Another entry shows the bishop's compassion for the villagers: 'Alms £3. 18s. for 18 poor amongst the customary tenants'. However, none of the holdings was vacant and the acreage of the demesne lands under cultivation was maintained unchanged both by the lord and the tenants who farmed it. Rents remained high. As the lord was short of labour the tenants were allowed to commute only a small fraction of their works, about a tenth, and only slightly over half of their ploughing dues. This state of affairs continued at any rate to Michaelmas 1351: from that date to October 1361 there are no records whatever.

Anyone leaving Downham in 1351 and returning there ten years later (as a reader of the rolls does) would find an entirely changed village. Many of the cottages and crofts had become badly dilapidated, some actually in ruins; eighteen of the customary holdings had fallen vacant and others were being let, temporarily, for money rents, a shilling an acre. Only 200 of the 400 acres of the demesne were being cultivated, half of this by the lord and half by the tenants who rented them – at reduced rates. The rest of the demesne and the assarted lands had gone to waste. The reeve's account for 1361/62 has a note: 'Fifty-two acres of customary land not let this year because of the lack of tenants: 341 acres of demesne land not let this year'.

This third and greatest depopulation of the place, this devastating change in ten years cannot be explained satisfactorily without contemporary records. There may have been much 'withdrawal from the manor' during the 1350s – by the poorer tenants going elsewhere in hopes of earning the high wages now being demanded and by the richer, successful tenants, tired of the restrictions of serfdom, and wanting to manage their own land, or other business, in their own way. Records for the later part of 1362 and for the following year, however, reveal that four of the eighteen tenants whose lands had become vacant had died in 1361. This is a high number for one year and other deaths may well have been shown on records which are missing, records earlier than that of March 1362 which has survivied. Even the known number of deaths suggests that yet another epidemic, the 'second pestilence', had attacked Downham.

During the 1360s the acreage of cultivated demesne land increased from about 200 to 300 and it was fairly evenly divided between lord and villeins. Rents remained at the pre-1346 rate. As the lord needed more labour for his increased acreage, very little commuting of services was allowed, only one-fifth of the 'works' and practically none of the ploughing. The letting of vacant holdings for money rents, free of services, continued to 1366, but then the clock was put back and tenants were again required, even ordered in court, to take holdings under the old terms. This naturally caused great discontent: in the court of 12 December 1376 the steward had to deal with flat refusals, by two tenants, to comply. The old order was not to change yet and serfdom was to continue.

A survey of the whole period of this study shows it in two sections: a century of prosperity to 1320, then half a century dogged by murrain, epidemic and plague, failures, abscondings and deaths. The over-population of the early years and a sturdy contending with their misfortunes later, kept the village as a going concern until the last fifteen, or perhaps twenty-five, years. The last troubles were the worst of all, but even so, the latest records show the village gradually returning to stability.

APPENDIX I

Rent Roll for Year 1369/70: 'Parcels of land let here in the 43rd Year'

at s. d.	from	Ac.	Roods		s.	d.
1 : 4	John Gaill		: 3	lying in the cultura between the mill &	1 :	
an acre	Geoffrey Buk	1 :		in same cultura [Redefinere	1 :	4
	Richard Snow	2 :		in same	2 :	8
	John Rote	1 :		in same	1 :	4
	Thomas Holt	2 :		in same	2 :	8
	John Biene	1 :	2	& a messuage in same	2 :	6
	John Wrongge		2	in same: granted at time of pestilence		8
at 1ˢ	Parson of Downham	6 :	2	abutting on Church, on south side	6 :	6
	John Wist	1 :		in cultura called le Churchill	1	
	Stephen Frost	1 :		in same cultura	1	
at s. d. 1 : 8	John Wyst, aforesaid	4 :		with messuage adjoining, for life	6 :	8
at 8d.	John Beneyt	13 :	1	in cultura called Shepehone	8 :	10
	Nicholas son of Simon	3 :		lying in Shepehone in Barlydon	2 :	
	John Verly	1 :	2	in Barlydon	1	
	John Colt		1	in same place		2
	Geoffrey Cardynal	2 :		in Holmhone	1 :	4
	Richard Whrite	1 :		in same cultura		8
	Stephen Frost	2 :		in same	1 :	4
	Thomas Holt	1 :	2	in same	1	
	Robert Persone's man	1 :		in same		8
	Simon Chetisham	1 :		in same		8
	William Hayt	6 :		in cultura called Stakehone	4	
	Robert Persone's man	1 :		in same cultura		8
	Richard Fox	1 :		in same		8
	Richard Snow	2 :		in same	1 :	4
	Geoffrey Cardynal	4 :		in same	2 :	8
	Richard Dokat	1 :	2	in same	1	
	John Rote	1 :		in same		8
	Thomas Holt	9 :		in same	6	
	William Shepherde	1 :		in same		8
	William Hayt	2 :	3	in same	1 :	10
	John Walsham	4 :	2	in same	3	
	Robert Monte	1 :		in same		8
	John Lovechild	2 :	2	in same	1 :	8
	Richard Whrite	1 :		in same		8
	Robert Rote	1 :		in same		8
	Hugo Prest	1 :		in same		8
	Isabell Bradwey Katerina Hunte	1 :	1	in same		10
	John Rote	1 :	2	in same	1	
	Adam Kede	2 :	2	in same	1 :	8
	William Veal	7 :		in same	4 :	8
	Reginald son of Adam Kede	1 :	2	in same	1	
	Robert Monte	1 :		in same		8
	Margaret widow of Richard Sinerles	1 :	3	in cultura next to Downham Hythe	1 :	2

97

APPENDIX I (continued)

		Ac.	Roods		s.	d.
at 8d.	Simon Sinerles	1 :		in same cultura		8
	Hugo Prest	2 :	2	in same	1 :	8
	John Sinerles Senior	1 :		in same		8
	do	3 :	1	in cultura called le Botine	2 :	2
	John Curteis	3 :	2	in same	2 :	4
	John Walsham	4 :		in same	2 :	8
	Robert Monte	1 :	3	in same	1 :	2
	Hugo Prest	1 :		in same		8
	Alan Draper	5 :		in same	3 :	4
	Richard Fox	1 :		in same		8
	Robert Rote	1 :		in same		8
	John Rote	1 :		in same		8
	William Veal	2 :		in same	1 :	4
	Adam Kede		1	in same		2
	Geoffrey Bridge	6 :		in same	4	
	Margaret Sinerles	1 :	2	in same	1 :	4
	Geoffrey Stoneye	3 :	2	in same	2 :	4
	John Rote junior	2 :		in same	1 :	4
	John, son of Ralph	1 :		in same		8
	Robert Rote	1 :	1	(sic) in cultura called le Heeth		8
	John Curteys	1 :		in same		8
	William Hayt	2 :		in same	1 :	4
	Nicholas, son of Simon	1 :	2	in same	1	
	Adam Kede		2	in same		4
	John, son of Ralph	1 :		in same		8
	Richard Snow		2	in same		4
	Simon Rote	3 :		of land called Acreland	2	
	Geoffrey Stoneye	1 :		in same		8
	Robert Rote	1 :		in same		8
	Rosa de Stoneye	1 :		in same		8
	Master John Cardynal Master of the Hospital of St John of Ely	1 :		in same		8
	Adam Kede	1 :		in same		8

APPENDIX II

Demesne Land taken by Tenants from Michaelmas 1373 for one year, for Sowing. [Extract from Court Roll: 1 December 1373]

In le Myddylhallecroft

Geoffrey Buk	1 acre of land	at 12d. an acre
Stephen Becher	2 acres	at 12d. an acre
Robert Rote	1 acre	at 12d. an acre
Alan Draper	1 acre, 1 rood	at 12d. an acre
John Hankyn	1 acre, 1 rood	at 12d. an acre

In le Netherhallecroft

William Warner	2 acres	at 12d.
William Dumfrey	1 acre, 1 rood	at 12d.
John Wrong	4 acres, 1 rood	at 12d.

Above Barlidonhone

John Fysshe, chaplain of Ely	11 acres, 3 roods	at 12d.

Above Parkehone

John Fysshe, chaplain of Ely	40 acres of warren	at 2s.

Over Cornedychone

John Fysshe, chaplain of Ely	7½ acres of land	at 2s.

Over Crouchone

John Shephyrd	1 acre, 1 rood	at 12d.
Simon Sinerles	2 acres	at 12d.
William Hayt	2 acres	at 12d.
Thomas Taylour	2 acres.	at 12d.
John Taylour	½ acre	at 12d.

Over Stakehone

John Walsham	1½ acres	at 12d.
Nicholas, son of Simon	4 acres	at 12d.
John, son of Ralph	1 acre	at 12d.
John Curteys	2 acres	at 12d.
John Rote	2 acres	at 12d.

Over Holmhone

Geoffrey Buk	2 acres	at 12d.
John Lovechyld	1 acre, 3 roods	at 12d.

Extract from the Fine Roll of 2 March 1329

1329
March 2
Grant to John de Hotham, bishop of Ely, and the prior and convent of Ely, out of devotion to the Virgin Etheldreda, whose body is buried in the church of Ely, and out of the king's special affection to the said John and for his good service to the king and his progenitors, and by assent of the prelates, earls, barons and other magnates of the realm that in every voidance of the bishopric of Ely the prior and convent shall have the guardianship of that bishopric and of the temporalities thereof, saving to the king's knights' fees held of the bishopric and advowsons of churches when they fall in in times of voidance. So that all rents and yearly services of those fees remain to the prior and convent, and saving also to the king's escheats falling in in times of voidance, so that all rents and yearly services thereof remain to the prior and convent, which escheats at the end of each voidance, to wit, after the elect has done fealty, shall be delivered to him: they rendering £2000 for each voidance if it last for a whole year and a proportionate sum for a lesser or greater period; and if the king cause his army to be summoned in time of voidance, the prior and convent shall not be held to do service therein for the proper and demesne knights' fees of the bishopric then in their hands, saving to the king the services of knights' fees held of the bishopric, and saving also the keeping of lands or rents acquired by bishops in fee hereafter, and of lands coming to the hands of bishops by escheat or otherwise, to be retained by escheators or other ministers during voidances, so that the rents and yearly services of such lands coming by escheat remain to the prior and convent and so that by reason of the keeping of such lands escheators or other ministers enter not the bishopric nor meddle therewith except to take simple seisin in the bishop's palace of Ely, staying there not more than one day.

SELECT BIBLIOGRAPHY

AULT, W.O.   *Open-field Farming in Medieval England: a Study of Village Bylaws.* (London, 1972)

BAGLEY, J.J.   *Historical Interpretation: Sources of English Medieval History, 1066–1540.* (Harmondsworth, 1965)

BAGLEY, J.J. and ROWLEY, P.B.   *A Documentary History of England, Vol. I (1066–1540).* (Harmondsworth, 1966)

BENTHAM, James.   *History and Antiquities of the Conventual and Cathedral Church of Ely.* (Cambridge, 1771)

Calendar of Fine Rolls

Calendar of Patent Rolls

CAM, H.M.   *The Hundred and the Hundred Rolls.* (London, 1963)

CAM. H.M.   *Liberties and Communities in Medieval England.* (London, 1963)

CHENEY, C.R.   *Handbook of Dates.* (Royal Historical Society, London, 1970)

DARBY, H.C.   *The Draining of the Fens.* (Cambridge, 1968)

DARBY, H.C.   *The Medieval Fenland.* (Newton Abbot, 1974)

DEWINDT, E.B.   *The Liber Gersumarum of Ramsey Abbey: a Calendar and Index of B.L. Harley MS 445.* (Toronto, 1976)

DUGDALE, William.   *The History of Imbanking and Drayning of Divers Fens and Marshes.* (London, 1662)

EKWALL, Eilert.   *The Oxford Dictionary of English Place Names.* (Oxford, 1960)

GODWIN, Harry.   *The Fenland: its Ancient Past and Uncertain Future.* (Cambridge, 1978)

HARDING, Alan.   *The Law Courts of Medieval England.* (London, 1973)

HECTOR, L.C.   *The Handwriting of English Documents.* (2nd edn., London, 1966)

HILTON, R.H.   *The English Peasantry in the Later Middle Ages.* (Oxford, 1975)

HOLMES, George.   *The Later Middle Ages, 1272–1485.* (London, 1970)

HOMANS, G.C.   *English Villagers of the Thirteenth Century.* (London, 1970)

HOWELL, M.E.   *Regalian Rights in Medieval England.* (London, 1962)

KERSHAW, Ian.   *The Agrarian Crisis in England, 1315–1322. In: Peasants, Knights and Heretics.* Ed. R.H. Hilton. (Cambridge, 1976)

LEVETT, A.E.   *Studies in Manorial History.* (London, 1962)

MAITLAND, F.W. (ed.)   *Select Pleas in Manorial and other Seignorial Courts. Vol. I: Reigns of Henry III and Edward I.* (Seldon Society Publications II, London, 1889).

MAITLAND, F.W. (ed.)   *The Court Baron.* (Seldon Society Publications IV, London, 1891)

McKISACK, May.   *The Fourteenth Century.* (Oxford History of England). (London, 1959)

MILLER, Edward.   *The Abbey and Bishopric of Ely.* (Cambridge, 1969)

MILLER, Edward and HATCHER, John.   *Medieval England: Rural Society and Economic Change 1086–1348.* (London, 1978)

MONCKTON, H.A.   *The History of English Ale and Beer.* (London, 1966)

MORGAN, Marjorie.   *The English Lands of the Abbey of Bec.* (London, 1946)

ORWIN, C.S. and ORWIN, C.S.   *The Open Fields.* (London, 1967)

OSCHINSKY, Dorothea (ed.).   *Walter of Henley: and Other Treatises in Estate Management and Accounting.* (Oxford, 1971)

PAGE, F.M.   *The Estates of Crowland Abbey: a Study in Manorial Organization.* (Cambridge, 1934)

POLLOCK, F. and MAITLAND, F.W.   *History of English Law.* (Cambridge, 1968)

POOLE, A.L.   *Obligations of Society in the Twelfth and Thirteenth Centuries.* (Oxford, 1946)

POSTAN, M.M. (ed.)   *The Cambridge Economic History of Europe. Vol. I: The Agrarian Life in the Middle Ages.* (Cambridge, 1966)

POWER, Eileen.   *The Wool Trade in English Medieval History.* (Oxford, 1941)

POWICKE, F.M.   *King Henry III and the Lord Edward: the Community of the Realm in the Thirteenth Century.* (Oxford, 1947)

POWICKE, F.M.   *The Thireenth Century, 1216–1307.* (Oxford, 1962)

RAFTIS, J.A.   *The Estates of Ramsey Abbey: a Study in Economic Growth and Organization.* (Toronto, 1957)

RAFTIS, J.A.   *Tenure and Mobility: Studies in the Social History of the Medieval Village.* (Toronto, 1964)

RAVENSDALE, J.R.   *Liable to Floods.* (Cambridge, 1974)

ROGERS, J.E.T.   *A History of Agriculture and Prices in England.* (Oxford, 1866)

Statutes of the Realm. Vol. I.   (London, 1810)

TITOW, J.Z.   *English Rural Society 1200–1350.* (London, 1969)

TITOW, J.Z.   *Winchester Yields.* (Cambridge, 1972)

TREHARNE, R.F.   *Essays on Thirteenth Century England.* (Historical Association, London, 1971)

TROW-SMITH, R.   *A History of British Livestock Husbandry.*   (London, 1957)

The Victoria History of the County of Cambridgeshire and the Isle of Ely. Vol. I. Ed. L.F. SALZMAN. (London, 1938)

The Victoria History of the County of Cambridgeshire and the Isle of Ely. Vol. IV. Ed. R.B. PUGH. (London, 1953)

VINOGRADOFF, Paul.   *Villainage in England.*   (Oxford, 1892)

ZIEGLER, Philip.   *The Black Death.*   (Harmondsworth, 1970)

GLOSSARY

Advowson	The right of presentation of a benefice.
Affeerors	Those (usually two) chosen by the court to assess the amounts of the amercements.
Agistment	1. The custom of taking, for payment, another owner's beasts to graze on one's land. 2. The price paid for the agisting.
Amercement	The sum imposed on one convicted in court: he is said to be 'in the mercy' of the court.
Assart	Land reclaimed from fen or woodland for cultivation.
Assize (of Bread or Ale)	The special court held once a year to ensure that the bread and ale sold in the vill were of the quality set by statute.
Barton	The home farm of the demesne.
Benefice	A church appointment, such as a rectory.
Book-hand	A script similar to the type of the earliest printers: used in books and for liturgical manuscripts.
Boon-work	Harvest work.
Camera	A private room.
Capon	A castrated cock.
Commissioners of Sewers	Appointed from the thirteenth century to improve the drainage of the fens and levy payment for the work.
Cotland	A holding of one acre in the fields.
Court-hand	An informal script used for business purposes, court rolls, etc. By the fourteenth century the letters were sometimes joined.
Coucher	'A large book such as remains lying for use on a desk or table. A large cartulary or register. Apparently from the Anglo-French *couchour*, he who lies, a lier'.[1] *The Coucher Book of Ely* is a book in which are bound all the extents of 1251 of the manors of the Bishop of Ely and other information concerning his property and that of the church (Charters, Grants, etc.).

1. *The Oxford English Dictionary*. (Oxford, 1933)

104

Cultura	A set of parallel strips in the open fields usually known as a furlong.
Customary Tenant	A tenant who, for his holding, must pay certain dues and perform certain services.
Demesne	That part of an estate occupied or cultivated by the owner.
Dorso	The reverse side of a roll.
Dredge	A mixture of barley and oats seed, sown as one crop.
Dyke-reeve	One elected by the court to serve under the Commission of Sewers and take charge of a particular dyke.
Extent	A document describing an estate and giving details of the tenants, their holdings, dues and services.
Farm (of mill, land, fishery, etc.)	The letting for a fixed period and for a fixed sum of money.
Feoffee	The person to whom a freehold estate in land is conveyed by a feoffment.[2]
Feoffment	The action of investing a person with a freehold estate in lands by livery of seisin.[3]
Firbôte	The tenant's right to take from common land wood for his home fires.
Frank-pledge	The system by which every member of a tithing was answerable for the good conduct of, or the damage done by, any one of the other members.[4]
Full Land	Fourteen acres of arable land in strips scattered in the fields.
Furlong	1. The length of a furrow ploughed. 2. A set of parallel strips in the field.
Gersuma	A tax, particularly the tax paid on entry into land.
Half Land	Seven acres: half a full land.
Headland	Land at each end of the arable strips, where the plough turned.
Heriot	Death duty in respect of customary tenants: the best beast in the case of a full-lander (or 16s.) and half that amount in the case of a half-lander.
Hogget	a yearling sheep.
Hokeday	The Tuesday following Low Sunday.

2. *O.E.D.*   3. *O.E.D.*   4. *O.E.D.*

Homage	The whole body of the court: every person present.
Hous-bôte	The tenant's right to take from common land wood for building or repairing his house.
Inquest	The enquiry to which a court case was submitted if the evidence was insufficient for decision.
Jury of Inquest	Twelve men elected to conduct an inquest and to report their findings to the court.
Jury of Presentment	Twelve men elected to present cases in court.
Lammas (O.E. *hlaf maesse: hlaf* = bread (loaf) + *maesse* = mass)	'The 1st of August . . . in the early English church observed as a harvest festival, at which loaves of bread were consecrated, made from the first ripe corn.[5]
Leet	An annual court held for the trial of lesser pleas of the Crown. The View of Frank-pledge and the Assize of Bread and Ale were amalgamated with it.
Lesch	Sedge (*Cladium mariscus*).
Leyrwite	A fine paid into court by a villein whose daughter had committed adultery.
Livery of Seisin	'The delivery of property into the corporal possession of a person; in the case of a house, by giving him the ring, latch, or key of the door; in the case of land, by delivering him a twig, a piece of turf, or the like.'[6]
Long Hundred	A hundred and twenty. A Danish reckoning which lingered to some extent in the Danelaw.
Mainpast	A dependent.
Mark	Thirteen shillings and fourpence.
Membrane	Oblong sheets of parchment, usually from the skins of sheep or goats.
Messuage	A house with its buildings and land.
Murrain	A term used to cover any diseases of horses, cattle and sheep.
Open fields	The arable fields of the vill, divided into furlongs and strips.
Pannage	1. The right to let swine forage in woodland. 2. The payment made for this right.
Pledge	One who stands pledge for another in court.

5. *O.E.D.*   6. *O.E.D.*

Presentment	The stating of a case against a defendent in court.
Reeve	The chief officer of the vill and an under-bailiff of the lord.
Regrate	To buy up market commodities, especially victuals, in order to sell them again at a profit in the same or a neighbouring market. 'The practice . . . was forbidden by various enactments.'[7]
Services	Customary duties to be performed by the holder of the land which bore those duties.
Sewers	Dykes for draining the fens.
Stot	A horse inferior to the cart-horses and used for ploughing with oxen.
Suit (of court, mill, etc.)	The attendance owed by villeins who were bound to attend the lord's court and to take their corn to be ground in the lord's mill.
Temporalities	The secular possessions of an ecclesiastic, rents, tithes, etc.
Tithing	A group of villeins (originally ten) mutually bound in the system of Frank-pledge and held responsible for each other's behaviour.
Tithing-man	The chief of a tithing: as a juror he presented the misdemeanours of his tithing in court.
Toft	An enclosure containing a house.
Turves	Squares of peat cut for fuel.
View of Frank-pledge	The court held (annually at Downham, with the leet) to review the system of Frank-pledge and to ensure that it was in working order.
Vill	The village or township.
Villein	One who held land in servile tenure, owing dues and services for his holding.
Villeinage	The status of a villein.
Withy	A branch of willow.
Works	The services due from the villeins to the lord in respect of their holdings.
Wytepund	A tax paid by every customary tenant and every cottager, possibly in commutation for services no longer rendered.

7. *O.E.D.*

TABLE I

Courts held in Reign of Edward II. Regnal Years 8/7/1307–20/1/1327

Membrane & Court Numbers	Date Given on Roll	Date of Saint's Day	Regnal Year	Bishop's Year	Date of Court	Type of Court	Later date in MS amended to earlier
I R 1	Mon. after Assumption	15 Aug	4	1	17/ 8/10	Admin. of Bylaw	Later date in MS amended to earlier
	Nativity BVM	8 Sept			14/ 9/10		
D 1	Tues. after S. Clement	23 Nov	4	1	24/11/10	Leet	
	Thurs. morrow of Ash Wednesday		4	1	25/ 2/11	Ordinary	
II R 1	Thurs. after SS. Peter & Paul	29 June	4	1	1/ 7/11	Ord	
D 1	Tues. after S. Matthew	21 Sept	5	2	22/ 9/11	Ord.	
III R 1	Tues. after S. Leonard	6 Nov	5	2	9/11/11	Leet	
D 1	Wed. after S. Wynewaldus	3 Mar	5	2	8/ 3/12	Ord.	
D 2	Mon. morrow of S. Barnabas	11 June	5	2	12/ 6/12	Ord	
D 3	Fri. in S. Michael	29 Sept	6	3	29/ 9/12	Ord	

Membrane is missing here. A court must have been held on Wednesday in Feast of S. Lucy 13/12/12, for reference is made to it in court held one year later, 13/12/13. There would probably be three more courts – in the spring, summer and autumn of 1313.

Membrane & Court Numbers	Date Given on Roll	Date of Saint's Day	Regnal Year	Bishop's Year	Date of Court	Type of Court	
IV R 1	Thurs. in S. Lucy	13 Dec	7	4	13/12/13	Leet	
R 2	Thurs. after Pentecost		7	4	23/ 5/14	Ord	
D 1	Tues. after S. James	25 July	8	4	31/ 7/14	Ord	
D 2	Tues. after S. Matthew	21 Sept	8	5	24/ 9/14	Ord	
V R 1	Tues. after St. Lucy	13 Dec	8	5	17/12/14	Leet	

VI	R	1	Mon. after S. Lucy	13 Dec	9	6	15/12/15	Leet	
	D	1	Fri. after S. Mathias	25 Feb	9	6	27/ 2/16	Ord	
			6½ years missing						
VII	R	1	Thurs. after Trans. S. Etheldreda	17 Oct	16	Not stated	21/10/22	Ord	
		2	Tues. after Conception BVM	8 Dec	16	–	14/12/22	Leet	
	D	1	Tues. after Nat. S. John Baptist	24 June	17	–	26/ 6/24	Ord	
		2	Tues. before S. Peter ad Vincula	1 Aug	18	–	31/ 7/24	Ord	3 essoins only.[1]
VIII	R	1	Mon. after S. Denis	9 Oct	18	–	15/10/24	Ord	
		2	Wed. before S. Thomas	21 Dec	18	–	19/12/24	Leet	
	D	1	Thurs. after S. John before Latin Gate	6 May	18	–	9/ 5/25	Ord	Two headings to this court.[2]
		2	Tues. after S. Matthew	21 Sept	19	–	24/ 9/25	Ord	
IX	R	1	Mon. after S. Lucy	13 Dec	19	–	16/12/25	Leet	
		2	Tues. after Conversion of S. Paul	25 Jan	19	–	28/ 1/26	Ord	
		3	Tues. after S. Mark	25 Apr	19	–	29/ 4/26	Ord	
	D	1	Wed. after S. Bartholemew	24 Aug.	20	–	27/ 8/26	Ord	
		2	Fri. after S. Matthew	21 Sept.	20	–	26/ 9/26	–	2 essoins only.[3]
X	R	1	Thurs. after S. Andrew	30 Nov	20	–	4/12/26	Leet	
		2	Thurs. after S. Scholastica	10 Feb	Not stated	–	12/ 2/27	Ord	
	D	1	Wed. in Vigil of Ascension	21 May	1	–	20/ 5/27	Ord	4 courts of the reign of Edward III. Regnal Years 25/1/1327–21/6/1377.
		2	Tues. morrow of S. Laurence	10 Aug	1	–	12/ 8/27	Ord	
		3	Fri. after S. Matthew	21 Sept	1	–	25/ 9/27	Ord	

1 No explanation for this.   2. Heading changed for superior saint.
3 Heading and essoins were entered in error on m IX d. They were intended for entry on m X d and appear there.

TABLE II

Courts held in Reign of Edward III. Regnal Years 25/1/1327–21/6/1377
For the first regnal year: see Courts of Edward II

Membrane & Court Numbers	Date Given on Roll	Date of Saint's Day	Regnal Year	Bishop's Year	Date of Court	Type of Court
I R 1	Thurs. after S. Andrew	30 Nov	1		3/12/27	Leet
2	Wed. after S. Peter in Cathedra	22 Feb	2		24/ 2/28	Ordinary
D 1	do					
	Fri. before S. George	23 Apr	2		22/ 4/28	Ord
	Thurs. in Translation of S. Thomas	7 July	2		7/ 7/28	Ord
	Tues. after S. Matthew	21 Sept	2		27/ 9/28	Ord
II R 1	Mon. after S. Andrew	30 Nov	2		5/12/28	Leet
2	Mon. before S. Valentine	14 Feb	3		13/ 2/29	Ord
3	Wed. before S. Dunstan	19 May	3		17/ 5/29	Ord
D 1	Tues. after Nativity of S. John Baptist	24 June	3		27/ 6/29	Ord
2	Tues. before S. Laurence	10 Aug	3		8/ 8/29	Ord
III R 1	Mon. after Nativity BVM	8 Sept	3		11/ 9/29	Ord
IV R 1	Wed. in Feast of S. Lucy	13 Dec	3		13/12/29	Leet
2	Wed. after Annunciation BVM	25 Mar	4		28/ 3/30	Ord
D 1	Thurs. after S. John before Latin Gate	6 May	4		10/ 5/30	Ord
2	Wed. after SS. Peter & Paul	29 June	4.		4/ 7/30	Ord
V R 1	Wed. after S. Matthew	21 Sept	4	14	26/ 9/30	Ord
VI R 1	Thurs. in S. Nicholas	6 Dec	4	15	6/12/30	Leet
2	Wed. before Purification BVM	2 Feb	4		30/ 1/31	Ord
D 1	Tues. after Palm Sunday		4		26/ 3/31	Ord
2	Fri. before S. Margaret, Virgin	20 July	5		19/ 7/31	Ord
3	Tues. after Nativity BVM	8 Sept	5		10/ 9/31	Ord

VII	R	1	Wed. after S. Andrew	30 Nov	5	16	4/12/31	Leet
		2	Fri. after S. Winwalocus	3 Mar	5		6/ 3/32	Ord
	D	1	Fri. morrow of Ascension		5		29/ 5/32	Ord
		2	Fri. in vigil of S. James	25 July	6		24/ 7/32	Ord
		3	Wed. after S. Matthew	21 Sept	6		23/ 9/32	Ord
VIII	R	1	Wed. after S. Andrew	30 Nov	6	17	2/12/32	Leet
		2	Wed. after Purification BVM	2 Feb.	7		3/ 2/33	Ord
		3	Sat. after Holy Trinity		7		5/ 6/33	Ord
	D	1	Sat. after S. Matthew	21 Sept	7		25/ 9/33	Ord
IX	R	1	Tues. in S. Clement	23 Nov	7		23/11/33	Leet
		2	Thurs. after S. Hilary	13 Jan	7		20/ 1/34	Ord
		3	Wed. after Ascension		7		11/ 5/34	Ord
		4	Mon. in S. Peter ad Vincula	1 Aug	8		1/ 8/34	Ord
	D	1	Wed. after beheading of S. John Baptist	29 Aug	8		31/ 8/34	Ord
X	R	1	Mon. after S. Katherine	25 Nov	8		28/11/34	Leet
		2	Wed. after S. Agatha	5 Feb	8		8/ 2/35	Ord
	D	1	Fri. morrow of SS. Peter & Paul	29 June	9		30/ 6/35	Ord
	D	2	Wed. in vigil of S. Matthew	21 Sept.	9		20/ 9/35	Ord
			Gap of 26 years					
XII	R	1	Wed. after S. Gregory	12 Mar	36	1	16/ 3/62	Ord
XIII	R	1	Wed. after SS. Peter & Paul	29 June	36		6/ 7/62	Ord
		2	Tues. after Nativity BVM	8 Sept	36		13/ 9/62	Ord
XI	R	1	Mon. before S. Nicholas	6 Dec	36	1	5/12/62	Leet
		2	Wed. before S. Gregory	12 Mar	37		8/ 3/63	Ord
		3	Mon. after Nativity S. John Baptist	24 June	37		26/ 6/63	Ord
	D	1	Thurs. after S. James, Apostle	25 July	37		27/ 7/63	Ord
	D	2	Fri. before S. Michael	29 Sept	37		22/ 9/63	Ord

TABLE II (continued)

Membrane & Court Numbers			Date Given on Roll	Date of Saint's Day	Regnal Year	Bishop's Year	Date of Court	Type of Court
XIV	R	1	Thurs. in Feast of S. Andrew	30 Nov	37		30/11/63	Leet
		2	Tues. before Conversion S. Paul	25 Jan	37		23/ 1/64	Ord
		3	Mon. after Invention of Holy Cross	3 May	38		6/ 5/64	Ord
		4	Sat. after S. Matthew	21 Sept	38		28/ 9/64	Ord
XV	R	1	Fri. after S. Fides	6 Oct	38		11/10/64	Ord
		2	Tues. after S. Andrew	30 Nov	38		3/12/64	Leet
		3	Fri. after S. Hilary	13 Jan	38		17/ 1/65	Ord
		4	Fri. after Annunciation BVM	25 Mar	39		28/ 3/65	Ord
	D	1	Fri. after SS. Philip & James	1 May	39		2/ 5/65	Ord
		2	Fri. after Translation of S. Thomas	7 July	39		11/ 7/65	Ord
		3	Tues. before S. Michael	29 Sept	39		23/ 9/65	Ord
XVI	R	1	Fri. after S. Edward, King	13 Oct	39		19/10/65	Leet
		2	Fri. after S. Lucy	13 Dec	39		19/12/65	Ord
		3	Fri. after S. Hilary	13 Jan	39		16/ 1/66	Ord
		4	Thurs. after S. Wynewaldus	3Mar	40		5/ 3/66	Ord
		5	Thurs. before S. Mark	25 Apr	40		23/ 4/66	Ord
	D	1	do					
		2	Tues. before S. Barnabas	11 June	40		9/ 6/66	Ord
		3	Thurs. in Mary Magdalene	22 July	40		23/ 7/66	Ord
		4	Fri. after Exaltation of Holy Cross	14 Sept	40		18/ 9/66	Ord
			Membrane missing					
XVII	R	1	Thurs. in Feast of S. Fides	6 Oct	41		7/10/67	Ord
		2	Mon. after S. Clement	28 Nov	41		29/11/67	Leet
		3	Thurs. after S. Hilary	13 Jan	41		20/ 1/68	Ord
		4	Thurs. after S. Mathias	25 Feb.	42		2/ 3/68	Ord
	D	1	Wed. after S. Mark	25 Apr	42		26/ 4/68	Ord
		2	Wed. before S. Augustine	26 May	42		24/ 5/68	Ord

112

XVIII	R	1	Mon. after SS. Peter & Paul	29 June	42		3/ 7/68	Ord
		2	Tues. after Exaltation of Cross	14 Sept	42		19/ 9/68	Ord
XIX	D	1	Fri. after S. Luke, Evangelist	18 Oct	42		20/10/68	Ord
		2	Tues. before S. Andrew	30 Nov	42		28/11/68	Leet
		3	Wed. after Epiphany	6 Jan	42		10/ 1/69	Ord
		4	Wed. in S. Valentine	14 Feb	43		14/ 2/69	Ord
		5	Thurs. before Annunciation BVM	25 Mar	43		22/ 3/69	Ord
	R	1	Fri. after Ascension		43		11/ 5/69	Ord
			Wed. after Translation of S. Thomas	7 July	43		11/ 7/69	Ord
XX	R	1	Thurs. after Exaltation of Cross	14 Sept	43		20/ 9/69	Ord
XXII	R	1	Thurs. after [hole in MS]	—			—	Leet
		2	Mon. after S. Wynewaldus	3 Mar	44		4/ 3/70	Ord
	D	1	Mon. after S. Dunstan	19 May	44		20/ 5/70	Ord
XXI	R	1	Mon. after S. James	25 July	44		29/ 7/70	Ord
		2	Mon. after Exaltation of Cross	14 Sept	44		16/ 9/70	Ord

Membranes missing

XXIII	R	1	Mon. after Nativity of S. John Baptist	24 June	47	Vacancy	27/ 6/73	Ord
		2	Mon. before S. Matthew	21 Sept	47		19/ 9/73	Ord
XXIV	R	1	Thurs. in S. Andrew	30 Nov	47	Vacancy	1/12/73	Leet
	D	1	Sat. after S. Winewalocus	3 Mar	48		4/ 3/74	Ord
XXV	R	1	Wed. after Trinity		48	1	31/ 5/74	Ord
		2	Fri. after S. Margaret	20 July	48		21/ 7/74	Ord
	D	1	Tues. before S. Matthew	21 Sept.	48		19/ 9/74	Ord

Membrane missing

TABLE II (continued)

Membrane & Court Numbers			Date Given on Roll	Date of Saint's Day	Regnal Year	Bishop's Year	Date of Court	Type of Court	
XXVI	R	1	Fri. in S. Andrew	30 Nov			30/11/75	Leet	
		2	Thurs. after S. Gregory, Pope	12 Mar	50		13/ 3/76	Ord	
	D	1	do						
XXVIII	R	1	Sat. after SS. Peter & Paul	29 June	50		5/ 7/76	Ord	
	D	1	Wed. after S. Matthew	21 Sept	50		24/ 9/76	Ord	
XXVII	R	1	Fri. after Conception BVM	8 Dec	50	3	12/12/76	Leet	
	D	1	Thurs. before S. Peter in Cathedra	22 Feb	51	3	19/ 2/77	Ord	
		2	Fri. before S. Margaret	20 July	1	4	17/7/77	Ord	1st Year of Richard II

114

No. of Roll	Period shown in Heading	Regnal Year	Bishop's Year	Year	Lord	Reeve
1A	Michaelmas to Friday following Purification BVM	*Ed. I* 29/30	–	1301/02	Vacancy	Simon Pope & Bailiff Tho. Sparkolp
1B	Tuesday before S. Margaret's Day to Michaelmas	29/30	1	1301/02	Robert of Orford	do
2	Michaelmas to Michaelmas	*Ed. II* 12/13	3/4	1318/19	John of Hotham	Richard Kede
3	do	13/14	4/5	1319/20	do	do
4	do	15/16	6/7	1321/22	do	William Stoney
5	do	16/17		1322/23	do	do
6	do	18/19	9/10	1324/25	do	do
7	do	*Ed. III* 1	11/12	1326/27	do	Simon Buk
8	do	2/3	13/14	1328/29	do	do
9	do	4/5	15/16	1330/31	do	do
10	do	5/6	16/17	1331/32	do	Simon Buk & Geoffrey Cardinal
12	S. Barnabas (11/6/37) to Michaelmas	10/11	1	1336/37	Simon of Montacute	Geoffrey Cardinal
13	Michaelmas to Michaelmas	15/16	5/6	1341/42	do	do
11	do	16/17	6/7	1342/43	do	do
14	do	17/18	7/8	1343/44	do	do
15	Michaelmas to 20 June	18/19	8/9	1344/45	Thomas de l'Isle	do
16	10 September to Michaelmas	18/19	1	1344/45	do	do
17	Michaelmas to Michaelmas	19/20	1/2	1345/46	do	do
18₁	do	20/21	2/3	1346/47	do	do
18₂	do	21/22	3/4	1347/48	do	do
18₃	do	22/23		1348/49	do	do
19	do	24/25	6/7	1350/51	do	John Dumfrey
20	do	25/26	7/8	1351/52	do	John Dumfrey & Geoffrey Cardinal
22	6 October to Michaelmas	35/36	17/18	1361/62	Simon Langham	Geoffrey Cardinal
23	Michaelmas to Michaelmas	37/38	19/20	1363/64	do	John Wrong
24	do	39/40	21/22	1365/66	do	do
25	do	41/42	23/24	1367/68	John Barnet	do
26	do	42/43	24/25	1368/69	do	do
27	do	48/49	30/31	1374/75	Thom. of Arundel	do

TABLE IV

Persons who broke the Assize of Bread

	Status	Date presented
1310–1334:		
John de Bredenham	Baker	1328
Cassandra Corner	Regrater	1315
Wife of Nicholas of Ely	Regrater	1315
Agnes Hasteler	Baker	1322, 1324, 1325
Joanna Hasteler (sister of Agnes)	Baker	1322
Robert Hasteler	Baker	1315
Agnes le Hunt	Regrater	1315
Alice Morris	Baker	1324, 1326, 1330, 1331, 1332, 1334
Agnes Pope	Alewife	1324
Emma Pope	Regrater	1315
Alicia Scut	Regrater	1333
Robert le Smyth	Baker	1328
Alice Stott	Regrater	1326
Christiana Sweyn	Baker	1326
Cassandra Woodward	Regrater	1315
1362–1376:		
'Stephen' [? Frost]	Regrater	1364

TABLE V

Brewers who broke the Assize of Ale 1310–1334

Name	1310	1311	1313	1314	1315	1322	1324	1325	1326	1327	1328	1329	1330	1331	1332	1333	1334
John Allen					+												
Robert Allen (wife of)				+													
Agnes wife of Walter the Brewster																+	+
Agnes Buk														+			
Beatrice Buk (known as 'Baldy Buk')	+	+	+	+	+	+	+	+	+	+	+			+	+	+	+
Margarita Buk																	+
Robert Buk				+													
Simon Buk								+									
Alice Cardinal			+														
Joanna wife of Hugo Cardinal													+				
Joanna wife of Simon Cardinal	+	+	+	+										+			
John Cardinal															+		
Agnes wife of Alan Carpenter			+	+	+												
Mabel Clement				+													
Agnes Cok																	+
John Cok												+					
Wife of John Cok						+											
Matilda Cok	+	+															
Isabella Columbers								+	+	+				+	+	+	+
Janyn Columbers						+											
John de Columbers												+	+				
Wife of John Columbers (brewer to the steward)							+										
Wife of William Dumfrey				+													
Margaret wife of John le Eyr							+	+	+	+	+						
Margery la Eyr						+											
Agnes le Fevere					+												
Robert le Fevere														+			
*Agnes Godelene																+	
Agnes le Hasteler							+	+	+	+	+	+		+	+	+	+
Robert le Hasteler					+							+	+				
Wife of Robert Hasteler	+		+	+													
Amicia atte Hythe		+															
Agnes Kede	+	+	+														
Alice Kede									+								
Margaret Kede														+			

*Also on Alewives' List

117

TABLE V (continued)

Date of Leet

Name	1310	1311	1313	1314	1315	1322	1324	1325	1326	1327	1328	1329	1330	1331	1332	1333	1334
Reginald Kede													+				
Margaret of March						+											
*Alice Morris							+		+		+						
Wife of Geoffrey Morris						+											
Isabel Morris							+										
Agnes Personn															+		
Juliana Personn														+			
William Personn								+									
Agnes le Plowright					+												
*Agnes wife of Thomas Pope	+		+				+		+	+	+			+	+		
Amicia wife of Simon Pope	+	+	+														
John Pope												+	+				
Katharine Pope	+	+		+			+	+	+	+	+						
*Margaret Pope								+	+	+	+						+
Thomas Pope						+						+	+				
Agnes of Pulham		+		+			+									+	+
Joanna of Quy					+												
John Rote	+																
Beatrice Sauser													+				
Wife of John Sauser	+		+														
Katherine le Sauser	+	+		+													
Wife of Geoffrey Scut			+														
Agnes wife of Robert le Smith	+	+	+	+		+	+	+	+	+							
Robert le Smith												+	+				
Matilda wife of Simon Starling	+																
Agnes de Stoneye															+		
Amicia de Stoneye														+	+		
Isabella de Stoneye								+									
Joanna de Stoneye			+	+		+	+				+			+	+	+	+
Wife of William Stoneye	+	+															
Agnes Stot		+															
Wife of Geoffrey Stot			+														
John of Stretham							+						+				
Wife of John of Stretham			+														
Agnes Wright	+																

* Also on Alewives' List

TABLE VI

Alewives who broke the Assize of Ale 1310–1334

Name	1310	1311	1313	1314	1315	1322	1324	1325	1326	1327	1328	1329	1330	1331	1332	1333	1334
Cecilia Bathoke		+															
Agnes Caurel							+										
Margaret of Doddington						+											
Amicia Dumfrey											+						
Agnes del Eth											+						
Beatrice le Feoffee					+												
Agnes Godalene																+	
Agnes la Hunt					+												
Amy Lavender		+															
Alice Morris							+										
Agnes Pelham		+															
Wife of Adam Pope					+												
Agnes Pope							+										
Margaret Pope									+								
Agnes Sinerles					+												
Mabel of Stoneye									+								
Cassandra Woodward		+	+														
Ibbota Woodward		+															

119

TABLE VII

Brewers and Alewives who broke the Assize 1362–1376

Name	1362	1363	1364	1365	1367	1368	1369	1373	1375	1376
Brewers:										
Amicia Bathoke								+		
Cecilia Brewster					+	+				
Alicia de Burgh				+						
*Agnes de Burton					+	+	+			
William Fish		+	+							
Alice Forman								+	+	+
Agnes Frost								+		
Cecilia Frost							+			
Stephen Frost					+	+	+	+	+	
*Cecilia Holt				+		+	+			
Stephen Holt										+
Thomas Holt					+					
William Janyn		+	+							
*Agnes wife of Wm. Janyn					+	+		+		+
*Agnes Morris		+	+							
Robert Morris					+					
Reginald de Pullerton					+					
Katerina Rote										+
Alice wife of John Sinerles					+		+	+		
Margaret Swan					+					
John Swyft							+			
Katerina Swyft						+		+		
Thomas Taylour									+	+
Simon atte Townsend				+	+					
Agnes Walsham								+		
*Alice Warner wife of William								+		
Alewifes:										
*Agnes de Burton								+	+	+
Margaret Durmodeys	+									
*Cecilia Holt	+									
*Agnes Janyn	+								+	
*Agnes Morris	+									
Margaret Snow				+						
*Alice Warner wife of William								+		+

* On both lists

TABLE VIII

Analysis of Surnames

	Christian name only	Patronymic 'son of'	Locative	Occupation or office (trade names)	Non-trade, 'real' surnames	Total
1222 Extent						
Customary tenants	13	6	1^a	1^e	2^n	23
Cottagers	4	4	–	6^f	8^p	22
Freemen	–	1	1^b	1^g	1^q	4
Total	17 (34.7%)	11 (22.4%)	2 (4.1%)	8 (16.3%)	11 (22.4%)	49
1251 Extent						
Customary tenants	1	10	1^a	4^h	14^r	30
Cottagers	1	7	–	3^i	10^s	21
Freemen	–	1	1^b	1^k	–	3
Total	2 (3.7%)	18 (33.3%)	2 (3.7%)	8 (14.8%)	24 (44.4%)	54
Court Roll 1310–1327	–	5 (3.0%)	37^c (22.3%)	39^l (23.5%)	85^t (51.2%)	166
Court Roll 1362–1370	–	2 (2.1%)	21^d (22.3%)	14^m (14.9%)	57^v (60.6%)	94

The letters a–v refer to the lists of names below.

Locative surnames

a   Stoneye

b   Leyton (or Longtown)

c   de Barton, de Berton, de la Bertone, de Burton, Brancaster, Bridge, de Carlton, de Chettisham, de Cottenham, Den(e)ver, de Doddington, Earith, Eastheth, de Grantesdun, de la Grene, de Hertecombe, atte Heth(e), atte Hill, de Hotham, atte Hythe, de Keten, de Leeton, de Merch, de Milbrok, de Norss, Overthewater, de Pulham, de Quy, de Shirburn, de Stoneye, de Stretham, atte Welle, de Wereham, de Wicheford, de Wymelington, de Wysett, de Wytewelle.

d   de Bedford, de Bele, de Berton, Bradeway, Bridge, de Brigham, de Burgh, de Cottenham, de Coveney, de Holt, de Holthum, de Isleham, de Kendale, de Kersey, Lynne, de Pulton, de Stoneye, atte Townsend, de Walpole, de Walsham, atte Wold.

Occupational and Trade Names

e   Reeve

f   Miller, Ploughman, Reeve, Smith, Swineherd, Weaver.

TABLE VIII (continued)

g   Clerk

h   Brewer, Carpenter, Hayward, Reeve.

i   Baxter (Baker), Smith, Swineherd.

k   Chaplain

l   le Barbour, le Baxter, Brewster, Carpenter, Carter, Chamberlain, Chaplain, Clerk Columbers, Cooper, Fisher, Fletcher, Gardener, le Gayte (watchman), Hasteler, Hay ward, Hendeman, le Hirde, le Hunt, Hunter, Mercator, Miller, Parker, Ploughwright Porter, Reeve, Sailor, le Sauser, Shearman, Shepherd, Smith, Sutor, le Taillour, Vache (cowman), Warrener, le Wayner, le Wayte (watchmen), Woodward, Wright.

m   Brewster, Cok (Cook), Cooper, Draper, Dykeman, le Hirde, Hunt, Miller, Page, Potter Shepherd, Smith, Tailor, Wright.

'Real' Surnames

n   Newman, Swanburger.

p   Ackerman, Biscop, Fox, Hart, Pope, Pecker, Prat, Tod.

q   le Grand

r   Barum, Buk, Cardinal, David, Ern–, Gonville, Kede, Morris, Newman, Osbern, Speak-well, Stott, Swanburger, Tod.

s   Alwyn, Barum, Bunting, Hayt, Petch, Pratt, Quincey, Rede, le Red, Tod,.

t   Alberd, Allen, Alred, Batayle, Bathoke, le Berch, Bolay, Brond, Bronn, Buk, Bunting, Caple, Cardinal, Cat, Caurel, Child, Chinnie, Conukhethen, Corner, Crisp, Daipersones, Daneth, Det, Dontessone, Dromideys, Dronnileys, Ducat, Dumfrey, Eliot, le Eyr, Faukes, le Feoffee, Ferour, Ficks, Fish, Fox, le Frankelyn, Freterurs, Frith, Gidhewer, Gill, Godeless, Godhewen, Hayt, Home, le Homice, Howet, Jacob, Kebbe, Kede, le Keu, King, Lark, Lavender, Lovechild, Lynde, Man, Manuneste, Maryat, Mayden, le Monner, Morice (Moryce, Moriz), Newman, Paste, Pelham, Personn, Pope, Prat, Prest, le Rede, Robelerod, Rote, Russell, Scut, Searle, Sinerles, Starling, Stott, le Straunge, Sumencer, Sweyn, Swon, Symondays, Valentine, Virli.

v   Alred, Bannesquynne, Bathoke, Benet, Bronn, Buk, Bunting, Cardinal, Chytom, Colvill, Culch, Curteys, Davy, Daggard, Deer, Deye, Dogit, Ducat, Dumfrey, Elyot, Fish, Fox, Frost, Godlimb, Hankin, Hayt, Jacob, Janyn, Kede, Lacy, Lavender, Long, le Longjohn, Lovechild, Maggison, Man, le Meyre, Morris, le Moy, Mynne, Pirde, Pope, Prest, Pykerell, Pypeshank, Rote, Rous, Scut, Sinerles, Snow, Spenser, Swan, Swift, Veel, Veyse, Wolfroan, Wrong.

TABLE IX

Bishops of Ely: 1220 to 1388

John of Fountains	1220	– 6/5/1225	died at Downham buried at Ely
Geoffrey de Burgh Archdeacon of Norwich	1225	– 17/12/1228	died
Hugh of Northwold Abbot of Bury St Edmunds	1229	– 6/8/1254	died at Downham buried at Ely
William of Kilkenny	1254	– 23/9/1256	died
Hugh of Balsham Sub-prior of Ely	*15/1/1258	– 16/6/1286	died at Doddington
John of Kirkby Canon of York	*7/9/1286	– 26/3/1290	died at Ely
William of Louth Dean of St Martins the Great	*30/5/1290	– 27/3/1298	died
Ralph of Walpole Bishop of Norwich	*10/10/1299	– 1302	died
Robert of Orford Prior of Ely	*4/2/1303	(on or before) – 19/1/1310	died at Downham
John of Ketton Monk of Ely (almoner)	*18/7/1310	(on or before) – 4/5/1316	died
John of Hotham Canon of York	*20/7/1316	(on or before) – 15/1/1337	died
Simon of Montacute Bishop of Worcester	*11/6/1337	(on or before) – 15/6/1345	died buried in Lady Chapel at Ely
Thomas de l'Isle Order of Friars Preachers	*10/9/1345	– 30/6/1361	died at Avignon
Simon Langham Abbot of Westminster	*19/3/1362	– 5/11/1366	Archbishop of Canterbury
John Barnet Bishop of Bath and Wells	*28/4/1367	– 7/6/1373	died at Hatfield
Thomas of Arundel Archdeacon of Taunton	*5/5/1374	– 1388	Archbishop of York

* Date of restoration of temporalities

TABLE X

A. Gersuma and Heriots paid on transfer of land: 1310–1335
[from Court Rolls]

		Date of Court (Month & Year)	Gersuma	Heriot	
On Full Lands: 10					
Family Transfers					
during life	1	9/35	29/-		
on death	6	5/25	3/4		
		2/28	26/5		
		7/28	N.S.	ox = 12/-	Late collection of heriot
		9/29	N.S.	horse = 10/-	
		7/31	40/-	1 mark	
		9/32	40/-		
Land Alientated	3	12/14	6/8	horse = 8/-	Land handed back for life: then to revert.
		2/16	20/-		Including leave to marry and enter holding.
		7/28	N.S.		
On Half Lands: 22					
Family Transfers					
during life	5	2/11	6/8		
		12/25	13/4		
		12/32	13/4		Including a cotland.
		2/33	excused		Transfer for 10 years. Including a cotland.
		6/35	10/-	½ ox = 6/8	Land handed back for life: then to revert.
on death	8	3/12	20/-	cow = 5/-	
		12/27	40/-		Via an alienation 'for life'.
		2/38	20/-	1 mark	
		4/28	40/-		
		9/29	N.S.	½ horse = 4/-	
		9/29	10/-	1/4	
		9/32	20/-		
		2/33	5/-	1/4	
Lands Alienated	9	12/14	13/4	1/4	Including a cotland and 2 acres enfeoffed land. Heriot collected 7/28, with others.
		6/15	6/8		Including leave to marry and enter the holding.
		5/25	10/-		
		12/26	20/-		Also 1/4 for 'leave to transfer'.
		2/28	30/-	10/-	

124

TABLE X (continued)

Date of Court (Month & Year)	Gersuma	Heriot	
7/28	N.S.	1/4	Late collection of heriots: see
7/28	N.S.	1/4	12/14 above.
9/29	30/-		
2/33	5/-		

)n Quarter Lands: 4

Family Transfers

during life	1	12/14	6/8		
on death	1	11/34	N.S.	¼ horse - 1/3	

Lands Alienated	2	7/28	N.S.	8d	Late collection of heriots.
		7/28	N.S.	8d	

)n Cotlands (less 5 already included with Half Lands and Quarter Lands): 14

Family Transfers

during life	4	9/15	3/4	
		6/24	3d	Including ½ acre and a dam.
		6/33	1/-	Including ½ cotland.
		6/35	1/-	
on death	3	2/16	13/4	
		9/32	6/8	
		31/8/34	1/-	
Alienated	7	9/15	N.S.	Including leave to marry daughter and enter holding.
		5/25	2/-	
		9/27	6d	Including 1½ acres adjoining.
		9/31	1/-	
		3/32	1/-	
		31/8/34	2/-	
		6/35	2/-	Including adjacent croft.

)n River Meadows: 5

Family Transfer (on death)	2	6/15	N.S.	
		7/11	6d	
Alienated	3	5/14	3d	
		7/14	2/-	Including ½ acre of land.
		9/27	2/-	

)n Fisheries: 9

New Fisheries	4	9/15	1/-	2d rent paid.
		9/15	6d	1½d rent.
		9/15	6d	½d rent.
		9/15	1/-	2d. rent.

TABLE X (continued)

		Date of Court (Month & Year)	Gersuma	Heriot	
Family Transfer	1	12/29	2/-		Including 1 acre of land and house.
Alienated	4	9/29	2/-		Including 1 acre of land.
		7/31	6d		
		9/32	excused		2d rent.
		11/33	6d		

On Houses (alone): 6

Family Transfer (on death)	1	3/32	3/4		
Alienated	5	2/11	3/-		
		12/22	1/3		
		3/32	10/-		
		9/32	3/4		
		2/33	3/4		

On Pieces of Land: 47

Family Transfer during life	3	5/29	1/-		1 rood enclosed in fen.
		12/29	1/-		6 sq. poles.
		3/32	1/-		33 x 53 ft.
on death	1	9/12	8/-		5 acres.
Alienated	43	11/10	6d		1 rood.
		2/11	1/-		3 x 1½ roods.
		5/14	6d		½ acre meadow.
		5/14	6d		½ acre meadow.
		12/14	1/-		¼ rood.
		6/15	N.S.		½ rood.
		12/15	6d		28 sq. poles.
		12/15	N.S.		do
		10/22	6/8		6 acres and house.
		12/25	1/-		16 sq. poles enclosed
		2/27	3d		1 acre.
		2/27	excused		½ acre.
		2/27	do		¼ acre.
		2/27	6d		3½ acres.
		2/27	3d		1 acre.
		2/27	3d		½ acre.
		2/27	1d		½ acre.
		2/27	6d		5 roods.
		2/27	6d		1½ acres.
		2/27	3d		5 roods.
		2/27	3d		½ acre.

Had been let, without leave, for 3, 4 or 5 harvests. Adjusted by payment of gersuma.

TABLE X (continued)

Date of Court (Month & Year)	Gersuma	Heriot		
2/27	6d		1 acre.	⎤ Had been let,
2/27	4d		¾ acre.	⎫ without leave,
2/27	6d		1 acre + ½ acre.	⎦ for 3, 4 or 5 harvests. Adjusted by payment of gersuma.
2/29	6d		28 sq. poles.	
7/30	N.S.		part of cotland.	
7/31	N.S.		½ acre demesne.	
7/31	N.S.		½ acre demesne.	
7/31	N.S.		5½ acres free land.	
7/31	1/-		9¼ acres free land.	
7/31	3d		1½ acres free land.	
9/31	1/4		1 acre 2½ roods.	
3/32	N.S.		N.S. 'land'.	
12/32	N.S.		5 acres free land.	
12/32	N.S.		5 acres.	
12/32	1/-		part of yard.	
12/32	1/-		curtilage.	
12/32	2/-		16 sq. feet.	
2/33	6d		6 acres Apesholt (assart).	
9/33	6d		1 acre and cottage.	
5/34	6d		3½ roods.	
11/34	1/-		10 sq. poles.	
2/35	1/6		7¾ acres demesne.	

TABLE X (continued)

B. Heriots paid at death: 1346–1352.
from Reeves' Stock Accounts for years 1346/47–1351/52 [D 10/2/18–20]

1346/47	Stephen Cardinal	1 stot worth 5/-
	Simon Personn	1 ox
	unnamed	1 foal
1347/48	William Lovechild	1 ox
1348/49	Richard Aleyn	1 stot
	John Columbers	half a stot
	Hugo le Brewster	1 ox
	Richard Mabbinson	1 ox
	John Buk	1 ox
	John Eliot	three-quarters of an ox
	Simon son of Mabel	half an ox
	John Aleyn	1 ox
	John Fox	three-quarters of an ox
1351/52	Simon son of Hugo	part of an ox

C. Gersuma paid on transfer of land: 1362–1377
[from Court Roll: no heriots entered in roll]

		Date of Court	Gersuma	
On Full Lands: 1				
Alienated	1	7/76	None	Vacant land taken up.
On Half Lands: 8				
Family Transfer				
during life	1	3/62	N.S.	Including 1½ cotlands. To pay 6/- p.a. for works
on death	1	3/62	2/-	Including a cotland for which to pay 4/- p.a. for works.
Alienated	6	5/65	N.S.	Including 1½ cotlands and bakehouse.
		9/66	1/-	Vacant land taken up.
		9/69	None	do
		9/69	None	do
		3/70	None	do
		3/70	3/7	For 12 years at 12/- p.a.

128

TABLE X (continued)

		Date of Court	Gersuma		

On Cotlands: 8

Alienated	8	6/63	8d	Vacant land taken up: for life at 3/- p.a.
		7/63	1/8	do	for lives of both.
		9/63	None	do (unwilling: *elected by homage*)
		5/64	10d	do	for lives: 4/- p.a.
		5/65	3d	do	for 10 years by services.
		10/67	6d	do	by services.
		9/69	None	do (unwilling: *elected by homage*)
		12/69	None	For 5 years: by services.

On River Meadows: 7

Family Transfers

during life	2	7/68	6d	Rent 1d. p.a. and by services.
		7/68	1/6	By services.
on death	1	4/68	2/-	Including house and fishery.

Alienated	4	5/68	6d		
		5/68	6/8	Rent 1d p.a.	Vacant land
		7/68	1/-	Rent 1d p.a. and services:	do
		7/76	N.S.	Including fishery: by services.

On Fisheries: 2

Alienated	2	12/62	N.S.	Vacant.
		5/68	9d	do

On Houses: 2

Alienated	2	3/62	1/-	
		7/62	40/-	Vacant. House and croft.

On Pieces of Land: 22

Family transfers

during life	1	3/70	N.S.
on death	1	7/76	N.S.

Alienated 20
Gersuma paid 5

		9/62	3d	Vacant land	Building and croft.
		9/62	3d		Eight sq. poles.
		9/62	2/6		Size not stated.
		10/65	3/4	Including a house	1 acre and a building.
		7/74	1/-	For life by services	4¼ acres.

No gersuma 15
shown

These include 4 vacant lands and 6 pieces of demesne land.
Demesne: 6½ ac. 2 at 6 ac. 4 ac. 1½ ac. 1 ac.
Vacant Lands: 4¼ ac. 1½ ac. 2 at 1 ac.
Others: 1¼ ac. ½ ac. ¼ rood and 2 size not stated.

TABLE XI

Acreage of Demesne farmed to Tenants or sown by the Lord

1 Roll Number	2 Year	3 Acres Farmed Out	4 Total	5 Wheat	6 Barley	7 Rye	8 Oats	9 Drage	10 Peas & Beans	11 Mixed Corn
						Acres sown by the lord				
		Acres Roods	Acres Roods	Acres Roods	Acres Roods	Acres Roods	Acres Roods	Acres Roods	Acres Roods	Acres Roods
1B	1301/02	–	–	*	40-0	–	66-0	–	12-0	–
2	1318/19	163-2	240-1	114-0	23-1	13-0	23-1	–	53-3	13-0
3	1319/20	163-2	212-0	74-0	34-3	–	74-0	–	30.0	–
4	1321/22	348-3½	112-0	49.0	19.0	–	–	–	44.0	–
5	1322/23	348.3½		*	32-0	42-0	–	–	–	–
6	1324/25	348-3½	110-0	46-0	32-2	5-0	–	–	26-2	–
7	1326/27	346-0	113-2	43-0	54-0	9.0	–	–	7.2	–
8	1328/29	255-2	151-1	67-2	51-2	2-0	14-1	–	16-0	–
9	1330/31	250-0½	181-3	71-0	54-1	10-0	7-2	–	32-2	6-2
10	1331/32	265-1½	177-3	75-1	61-1	1-0	3-0	7-0	30-1	–
12	1336/37	268-2½	152-3	50-3	55-0	19-0	4-0	–	24-0	–
13	1341/42	270-0½	177-0	54-2	60-2	11-2	13-1	–	37-1	–
11	1342/43	270-0½	160-1	55-0	54-0	14-0	4-1	–	33-0	–
14	1343/44	270-0½	163-0	65-0	53-1	10-0	8-3	–	26-0	–
15 & 16	1344/45	270-0½	163-3	51-0	55-0	12-0	13-2	–	32-1	–
17	1345/46	276-1½	155-2	50-0	55-0	12-0	4-2	–	34-0	–
18_1	1346/47	276-1½	137-3	48-2	48-2	7-2	4-2	–	28-3	–
18_2	1347/48	276-1½	147-0	52-0	42-0	10-0	–	–	43-0	–
18_3	1348/49	276-1½	140-2	43-0	46-1	12-1	0-2	–	38-2	–
19	1350/51	276-1½	150-1	42-0	42-0	9-3	–	12-0	44-2	–
20	1351/52	276-1½	139-0	47-0	39-0	16-2	–	–	36-2	–
22	1361/62	107-2	*	*	*	*	*	*	*	*
23	1363/64	88-2	117-0	30-0	25-0	14-0	21-0	10-0	17-0	–
24	1365/66	125-3	127-0	56-0	42-0	–	10-0	–	19-0	–
25	1367/68	151-3	113-0	52-0	32-0	–	15-0	–	14-0	–
26	1368/69	157-3	138-0	43-2	52-0	–	20-0	–	22-2	–
27	1374/75	Much of this account is torn away.								

* Illegible.

Note: Column 3 is taken from the credit portion of the Money Account (Reeves' Accounts)
Columns 5–11 are taken from the Grain Account (Reeves' Accounts)

Also: 1369/70   162-2   is shown in the Rent Roll for 1369/70 (Appendix I)
1373/74   95-2   is shown in the Court Roll (Appendix II)
for one year

130

TABLE XII

Rents of Demesne Land farmed to Tenants

1	2	3	4	5	6	7	8	9	10	11		
						Rent per acre						
Roll No.	Year	Total acres	8d	1s	1s 4d	1s 6d	1s 8d	2s	2s 6d	Total rents		
		Ac R	Ac R	Ac R	Ac R	Ac R	Ac R	Ac R	Ac R	£	s	d
2	1318/19	163-2		123-1½		14-3		12-2	12-3½	10	2	8½
3	1319/20	163-2		123-1½		14-3		12-2	12-3½	10	2	8½
4	1321/22	348-3½		308-3		14-3		12-2	12-3½	19	8	0¾
5	1322/23	348-3½		308-3		14-3		12-2	12-3½	19	8	0¾
6	1324/25	348-3½		308-3		14-3		12-2	12-3½	19	8	0¾
7	1326/27	346-0		308-3		14-3		10-2½	11-3½	19	1	9¾
8	1328/29	255-2		218-1		14-3		10-2½	11-3	14	11	0
9	1330/31	250-0½	211-1	14-3	12-1		11-3½			9	10	1½
10	1331/32	265-1½	226-0	14-3	12-1		12-1½			9	19	9
12	Part 1336/37	268-2½	229-1	14-3	12-1		12-1½			5	2	3¼*
13	1341/42	270-0½	230-3	14-3	12-1		12-1½			10	5	6½
11	1342/43	270-0½	230-3	14-3	12-1		12-1½			10	5	6½
14	1343/44	270-0½	230-3	14-3	12-1		12-1½			10	5	6½
15 } 16	1344/45	270-0½	230-3	14-3	12-1		12-1½			7	14	1¾**
17	1345/46	276-1½	237-0	14-3	12-1		12-1½			10	9	8½
18¹	1346/47	276-1½		237-0		14-3		12-1	12-1½	15	14	6¾
18²	1347/48	276-1½		237-0		14-3		12-1	12-1½	15	14	6¾
18³	1348/49	276-1½		237-0		14-3		12-1	12-1½	15	14	6¾
19	1350/51	276-1½		237-0		14-3		12-1	12-1½	15	14	6¾
20	1351/52	276-1½		237-0		14-3		12-1	12-1½	15	14	6¾
22	1361/62	107-2	54-0	48-0	5-2					4	11	4
23	1363/64	88-2	86-0	2-2						2	19	10
†24	1365/66	125-3	111-0	6-2	8-1					4	11	6
†25	1367/68	151-3	125-0	14-0	8-3		4-0			5	15	8
†26	1368/69	157-3	133-0	11-2	7-3		5-2			5	19	8
†27	1374/75	132-0	121-2	5-0	1-2		4-0			4	14	8

Columns 4 to 11, above, are taken from the credit side of the reeves' money accounts.

* Two quarterly payments only.

** Three quarterly payments only.

† See note on p. 132.

TABLE XII (continued)

The accounts for these four years give fuller details and show the actual location of some of the acres farmed:

1365/66	at 1/-	6½ acres.	2½ near the mill: 4 near the church.
1367/68	at 1/-	14 acres.	2½ near the mill to John Dene
			3 near the church
			6 against the church, to the parson for 8 years
			¼ in the cultura near the church to John Swift (in the cultura called le Hull)
	at 1/8	4 acres.	to John Swift with a messuage.
1368/69	at 8d		8 to John Benet in cultura Shephone
	at 1/-		3 near church, 6½ near church to parson, 1 in le Hull to John Swift, 1 to Stephen Frost.
	at 1/4		1½ near mill to John Dene for life as in court roll
			4 with messuage to John Day for life, ½ to John Strong (near Redifinere)
1374/75	at 1/-		4 to parson, 1 to Stephen Frost
	at 1/4		1½ next to mill, to John Dene
	at 1/8		4 to John Swift, for life

TABLE XIII

Jurors: 1310–1334

Status	Name	24/11/10	9/11/11	13/12/13	17/12/14	15/12/15	16/12/25	4/12/26	3/12/27	5/12/28	13/12/29	6/12/30	2/12/32	23/11/33	28/11/34	Reeve's a/c or Court reporting death
FL	Richard Aleyn														+	D10/2/18³ 48/49
©	Robert Aleyn										+	+	+	+		
	John of Brancaster		+													
FL	Richard Buk												+	+	+	
FL	Robert Buk				+											Ed.III 9/5/25
®FL	Simon Buk	+	+	+	+	+	+	+	+	+						
®HL	Geoffrey Cardinal													+	+	
FL	Hugo Cardinal												+	+	+	
®FL HL	Simon Cardinal	+	+	+	+	+	+	+	+	+	+					Ed.III 19/7/31
	William Cardinal	+														
FL	Robert the Carter		+	+	+	+	+	+	+							
	Roger the Clerk		+													
HL	John Cok	+	+	+	+	+	+	+	+	+	+	+	+	+		
HL	John Columbers								+	+	+	+	+	+	+	D10/2/18³
	Maurice Daneth	+														
HL	Ralph Eliot	+			+											
	Robert Earith	+														
	William Ficks		+													
	Reginald Kede									+	+	+	+	+	+	
®©	Richard Kede	+	+	+	+	+	+	+	+	+	+	+	+		+	
	Simon Kede				+							+				
	John Lovechild	+			+											
	Simon Malleson													+		
FL	Simon Personn													+		
®FL HL ©	William Personn		+	+	+		+	+	+	+						Ed.III 11/9/29
	Adam Pope	+														
®HL ©	Simon Pope		+	+	+		+	+								
©	Thomas Pope		+	+	+	+	+	+	+	+	+	+	+	+	+	
©	John Rote	+	+	+	+											
HL	John le Sauser	+	+			+										
HL	Simon le Sauser						+	+	+	+	+	+	+	+	+	
HL	Geoffrey Scut			+	+	+	+	+	+	+	+	+	+	+	+	
©	Robert the Smith						+	+	+	+	+	+	+		+	
FL	Simon Starling	+	+	+	+											
®FL	William of Stoneye		+	+	+		+	+	+	+	+	+				
½©	John Stott	+														
	John of Wereham		+													

®= Reeve (at some time) FL = Full Land holder HL = Half Land holder ©= Cotlander

TABLE XIV

Jurors: 1362–1377 (a: 1362–1366)

Status	Name	16/3/62	30/11/63	28/9/64	11/10/64	3/12/64	17/1/65	28/3/65	2/5/65	11/7/65	17/10/65	19/12/65	16/1/66	5/3/66	23/4/66	9/6/66	23/7/66	18/9/66
HL	Geoffrey Buk	+	+	+	+	+	+	+	+	+	+	+			+	+	+	+
	John Buk																	
®FL	Geoffrey Cardinal																	
FL	John Cok	+		+	+	+	+	+	+	+	+	+	+	+	+	+	+	+
	Alan Draper																	
	William Dumfries																	
	Geoffrey Elyot																	
HL	Stephen Frost																	
	John Hankyn		+		+	+					+	+						
®FL©	William Hayt	+	+		+	+				+	+	+	+	+	+	+	+	+
	Geoffrey Holt																	
HL	William Janyn	+		+	+		+						+	+	+			
	Adam Kede	+	+	+	+	+	+	+	+	+	+	+	+				+	+
HL	Richard Kede																	
HL©	Simon Kede																	
®FL	John Lovechild	+	+	+	+	+		+			+	+						
©	Robert Moriz	+	+	+	+	+	+	+	+	+	+	+	+	+	+	+	+	+
FL	Geoffrey Ponte															+	+	
	Hugo Prest	+	+		+	+	+	+	+	+	+	+	+	+				+
HL	John Purde																	
HL	John Rote		+															
HL	Robert Rote																	
HL	Simon Rote																	
	John Sinerles	+		+						+	+	+		+	+	+	+	+
	Richard Sinerles															+		
¾L HL	Simon Sinerles			+									+	+		+	+	+
HL©	William Skut																	
HL	Geoffrey Stoneye	+	+	+	+	+	+	+	+	+	+	+	+	+	+	+	+	+
HL	John Stoneye			+	+		+	+	+	+			+	+	+			
	Richard Snow					+	+	+	+				+	+	+		+	+
®FL S40	Nicholas son of Simon	+	+	+	+	+	+	+	+	+	+	+	+	+	+	+	+	+
HL	Simon atte Townsend	+	+		+	+	+	+	+	+						+	+	+
	William Veal																	
	John Walsham																	
	Simon Wright			+								+			+			
®FL S20	John Wrong		+			+						+	+					

® Reeve at some time (from Court Rolls & Headings of Accounts)

FL = Full Land holder
HL = Half Land holder
¾ L = ¾ Land holder
© = Cotlander
S = known to have owned sheep (at least 40/20)
} from Court Rolls

TABLE XIV (continued)

Jurors: 1362–1377 (b: 1367–1370)

Status	Name	7/10/67	29/11/67	20/1/68	2/3/68	26/4/68	24/5/68	3/7/68	19/9/68	20/10/68	28/11/68	10/1/69	14/2/69	22/3/69	11/5/69	11/7/69	–/12/69*	4/3/70
HL	Geoffrey Buk	+	+	+		+	+	+	+	+	+	+	+	+	+	+	+	+
	John Buk																	
®FL	Geoffrey Cardinal							+	+	+						+		
FL	John Cok	+	+	+	+	+	+	+	+	+	+	+	+	+	+	+	+	+
	Alan Draper																	
	William Dumfries					+												
	Geoffrey Elyot				+													
HL	Stephen Frost							+	+	+								
	John Hankyn																	
®FL ©	William Hayt	+	+								+	+	+	+	+	+		+
	Geoffrey Holt																	
HL	William Janyn			+	+		+											
	Adam Kede	+	+	+	+	+		+	+	+	+	+	+	+	+	+	+	+
HL	Richard Kede																	
HL ©	Simon Kede																	
®FL	John Lovechild	+	+	+	+			+	+	+	+	+	+	+	+	+	+	+
©	Robert Moriz	+	+		+	+						+	+	+	+		+	+
FL	Geoffrey Ponte					+												
	Hugo Prest	+	+	+	+	+		+	+	+	+	+	+	+	+			+
HL	John Purde					+												
HL	John Rote					+												
HL	Robert Rote																	
HL	Simon Rote							+	+	+								
	John Sinerles	+	+	+	+	+	+											
	Richard Sinerles																	
¾L HL	Simon Sinerles							+										
HL ©	William Skut																	
HL	Geoffrey Stoneye	+	+	+	+	+	+	+	+	+	+	+	+	+	+	+	+	+
HL	John Stoneye	+	+	+	+	+	+					+	+	+	+	+	+	+
	Richard Snow	+	+	+	+	+		+	+	+						+		
®FL S40	Nicholas son of Simon			+	+			+	+	+	+	+	+	+	+	+	+	+
HL	Simon atte Townsend											+	+	+	+			
	William Veal																	
	John Walsham																	+
	Simon Wright	+	+	+	+	+		+	+	+					+	+		+
®FL S20	John Wrong									+	+	+	+	+	+	+		

*Names of 3 jurors torn off MS.

TABLE XIV (continued)

Jurors: 1362–1377 (c: 1370–1377)

Status	Name	20/5/70	29/7/70	27/6/73	19/9/73	1/12/73	4/3/74	21/9/74*	19/9/74	30/11/75	13/3/76	5/7/76	24/9/76	12/12/76	19/2/77	17/7/77	Court reporting death
HL	Geoffrey Buk	+	+	+	+	+	+	+	+	+	+	+	+	+	+	+	
	John Buk		+	+								+	+	+			
®FL	Geoffrey Cardinal		+	+					+	+		+	+	+			
FL	John Cok	+	+	+	+	+	+	+	+	+	+	+	+		+	+	
	Alan Draper											+	+	+			
	William Dumfries																
	Geoffrey Elyot																
HL	Stephen Frost																
	John Hankyn																
®FL ©	William Hayt	+	+	+	+	+	+	+	+	+	+	+	+	+	+	+	
	Geoffrey Holt										+						
HL	William Janyn																E.III 4/3/74
	Adam Kede	+	+	+	+		+		+	+	+	+	+	+	+	+	
HL	Richard Kede					+		+									
HL ©	Simon Kede											+	+	+			
®FL	John Lovechild	+	+			+	+	+	+	+	+	+	+	+	+	+	
©	Robert Moriz	+	+	+	+	+	+		+	+				+	+	+	
FL	Geoffrey Ponte																
	Hugo Prest	+		+	+	+			+	+				+	+	+	
HL	John Purde		+														
HL	John Rote		+														E.III 5/7/76
HL	Robert Rote			+	+	+	+		+	+	+	+	+	+	+	+	
HL	Simon Rote																
	John Sinerles		+														
	Richard Sinerles																
¾L HL	Simon Sinerles																
HL ©	William Skut												+	+			
HL	Geoffrey Stoneye	+	+	+	+	+	+	+		+	+	+	+	+	+		
HL	John Stoneye	+															
	Richard Snow																
®FL S40	Nicholas son of Simon	+		+	+	+	+	+	+					+	+	+	
HL	Simon atte Townsend			+	+	+	+	+	+								
	William Veal		+														
	John Walsham	+	+				+								+	+	
	Simon Wright	+									+			+	+	+	
®FL S20	John Wrong							+	+	+	+	+		+			

* Names of two jurors torn off MS

TABLE XV

Schedule of Land Transfers (for key see p. 155)

Date*	Description of land	Conditions of holding	First owner	Second owner	Gersuma s	d	Heriot s	d	
14/9/10	F (between Manea and Coveney)		Maurice of the Hythe John & Agnes Bridge	—					
29/11/10	1 rood		Cassandra of the Hythe	Thomas of Lecton					
25/2/11	H.L.		Agnes Bridge & son John	William Bridge (son)		6		8	Agnes to hold for her life. At her death to revert to William.
	M	1d a year	Richard the fletcher	John Daepersonnes		3			To hold for self & heirs by villein tenure for rent of 1d a year.
	Plot: 3 roods x 1½ attached to above M	½d a year	Simon Pope	do		1			do do ½d pa
1/7/11	R.M.		Juliana the gardener	Simon Pope		6			
8/3/12	H.L. & house		Richard Cock (died)	John Cock (son)		20			Best cow Proved nearest heir. = 5/-
29/9/12	M & 5 acres		Isabel Pope (died)	Adam Pope (son)		8			
23/5/14	½ acre in le Parokhone	6d pa	Simon Buk	Simon Cardinal junior				6	To hold at the lord's will.
	½ acre above Barleydonehone	6d pa	Simon Cardinal junior	Simon Buk				6	do
	R.M. in West Fen between those of Simon Pope & Simon Cardinal		Juliana the gardener	John Hayt				3	To hold for self & heirs.
31/7/14	R.M. in common fen at Downham Hythe	12d pa	[received from the lord]	John Sinerles		2			do
17/12/14	Part of holding: 4 x 2 perches	½d pa	Adam of Chettisham	William Starling		1			To hold at the will of the lord. To pay to Adam & his heirs 12d pa at 4 seasons of year.

TABLE XV (continued)

Schedule of Land Transfers

Date*	Description of land	Conditions of holding	First owner	Second owner	Gersuma (s d)	Heriot (s d)	
	F.L. & house		Robert the carter & wife Alice	Simon Pope	6 8	Horse = 8/-	Land was Alice's dowry from previous marriage with Richard the carter. Robert & Alice to hold land for their lives: then land to revert to Simon.
	Q.L. & part C & M (+ 1 acre enfeoffed)		John Kebbe	Richard Kebbe (brother)	6 8		John to hold for life the part C & M + part of the acre; land then to revert to Richard.
	H.L. & M & C (+ 2 acres enfeoffed)		Richard Kebbe	William Personn	13 4	1 4	
18/6/15	H.L. & M		Amicia, widow of Adam, son of Peter of the Hythe	Hugo, son of Nicholas the shepherd	6 8		The fine was for licence to marry Amicia & enter her holding.
	½ rood from her messuage 6 x 3 perches	1 hen at Christmas	Isabella widow of Clement Stott	Robert son of William the Sauser	Not stated		To hold for self & heirs in villeinage
	R.M. (1 rood)		Reginald Sinerles	John Sinerles (brother)	do		To hold in villeinage.
	F at Sidditch		Juliana the gardener	William of Stoneye	do		
23/9/15	½C (½ acre)		William, son of Alexander Virli	Alexander Virli & 2nd wife Agnes & daughter Agnes	3 4		Formal surrender of land which would come to him on his father's death, as his inheritance from his mother Margaret Virli decd.
	C	2d pa	Clement Stot	Hugh son of John, carter	Not stated		For leave to marry Clement's daughter, Amicia & to hold the C.
	F: Haytesdam to corner of park		[received from the lord]	Robert, son of Richard le Ken	1		To hold for self & heirs in villein tenure.
	F: Haytesdam to	1½ pa	do	Clement the	6		do

Date	Land / Description	Rent / Payment	Grantor	Grantee					Notes
	to dam of Robert Morris F: Robert Morris' dam to Sidditch		do	Robert le Sauser	1				do
15/12/15	7 x 4 perches of his messuage	½d pa to lord, 4d pa to William	William of Stoneye	Robert Hasteler & Agnes his wife		6			Formal surrender of any right or claim to the land.
	The same piece of land	2d pa	Robert le Sauser & his wife Joanna of Stoneye	do					Proved nearest heir.
27/2/16	C		Maurice of the hythe (died)	Simon, his son	13	4			
	FL		Agnes, widow of Adam John Buk the carpenter		20				For leave to marry the widow & for entry into the land.
21/10/22	M & 6 acres		Richard Eliot	Richard Kede	6	8	1	4	Kede to hold after Eliot's death. Meanwhile Kede to hold part of it for crops & pay Eliot 200 sedges & 500 turves a year. Eliot to hold & cultivate the rest & give Kede all the resulting dung.
14/12/22	M		Henry Corner	Julia, daughter of John the brewer	1	3			
26/6/24	C & 1 rood in Snakeland, 1 rood in Hankele, part of a dam in the fen		Simon Pope	Thomas Pope	3				
9/5/25	C		Richard Kede	Agnes, daughter of Thomas of March	2				
	F.L.		Robert Buk (died)	Anita, his daughter	3	4	Not stated		Proved age 21
16/12/25	H.L.		Anita Buk	Simon Sauser	10				
	H.L.		Simon Cardinal	Geoffrey Cardinal (son)	13			4	Simon to hold until his death & to render dues & services.
	Enclosed land 4 x 4 perches		Simon Pope	John de Columbers	1				For self & heirs at the will of the lord.
4/12/26	H.L. & house		William Dunfrey & Amicia his wife	William, son of Philip Lovechild	20		1	4	Heriot paid for leave to alienate land.

TABLE XV (continued)

Schedule of Land Transfers

Date*	Description of land	Conditions of holding	First owner	Second owner	Gersuma s	Gersuma d	Heriot s	Heriot d	
12/2/27	1 acre		Robert Allen	John le Eyr (freeman)		3			For 3 harvests
	½ acre		Juliana the gardener	William of Hotham	Excused				
	¼ acre		Cecilia Bathoke	do	Excused				The juror presented that these transactions had been made in the past without leave. The matters were now adjusted by payment of fines 'for leave to hold the said land'.
	¼ acre		John Man	Philip Lovechild		6			For 5 harvests
	3½ acres		do	Adam Buk		3			For 3 harvests
	1 acre		do	Agnes Scut		3			do
	½ acre		do	Geoffrey Smith		1			
	1¼ acres		Hugh Shepherd	Philip Lovechild		6			For 3 harvests
	1½ acres		do	Geoffrey Smith		6			do
	1¼ acres		do	Simon Buk		3			do
	½ acre		do	Adam Buk		3			do
	1 acre		Simon Warren	Geoffrey Scut		6			For 4 harvests
	¾ acre		Simon Kede	Adam Buk		4			do
	1 acre		John Child	Nicholas Scut		6			do
	½ acre			do					
25/9/27	C & 1½ acres adjoining it		Robert Smith	Agnes Rote & John (eldest son)		6			To hold for 6 years & live in adjacent yard, Robert to perform all dues & services.
	R.M.		Nicholas Scut & wife Emma	Robert del Brook	2				R.M. once belonged to Adam Spendelove. This court was held by Nicholas, 'steward of the justices of Ely'.
3/12/27	½ C & 1 acre		Isabella Morris	John Stot & wife Joanna	2				
	H.L. & ¾ M		Simon Pope (died)	John son of Wm. Brewster	40				Land formerly belonged to William Brewster, father of John. William died & Simon Pope held the land for the duration of his life.

Date	Former tenant	Heir / new holder	Age	Heriot	Land & tenure	Notes
24/2/28	Matill widow of Simon Starling (died)	William Starling (son)	26	8	F.L. & M	It was acknowledged that son & heir of Simon should inherit.
	Nicholas Scut (died)	Geoffrey Scut (brother)	20	½ ox	H.L. & M	It was acknowledged that brother & heir of Nicholas should inherit.
	Geoffrey Scut	John, son of Geoffrey the smith	30	10 (half share)	same land & M	John to pay Geoffrey Scut (for duration of Geoffrey's life) 2 qr. wheat, 2 qr. barley, ½ qr. beans & peas, p.a. at 4 seasons of the year. Land held by Katerina for her life after death of her husband.
22/4/28	Katerina, widow of John le Sauser (died)	Richard (grandson)	40		H.L.	
7/7/28	Simon Cardinal	John Cardinal (son)		1	F.L. & M	ox = 12/- The jurors made a report on heriots (4) that had been paid in past years (4) (going back to 1314). They (8) reported nine cases, but only these (8) five, which must have appeared on (8) membranes now missing, are copied here. The others appear on their proper dates.
	Simon Codholben	John Columbers		1	H.L.	
	William Bridge	John Cok			H.L.	
	Geoffrey Moriz	Henry Sauser			Q.L.	
	Robert Moriz	Geoffrey Smith			Q.L.	
13/2/29	Etheldreda dau. of John Dolre	William of Stoneye			F.L. & M	Land & messuage held by the lord until ingress money settled.
17/5/29	Simon Cardinal	John Hayt			F.L. & 7 x 4 perches	
	John Sinerles	Henry Sinerles		6	1 rood (enclosed)	
	not named (freeman)	Geoffrey Scut		1	3¾ acres	These transactions came to light at an inquest concerning lands & tenements bought by villeins from freemen.
In the past. Dates not given	do	Adam Buk			5 acres	
	do	Geoffrey the Smith & his daughter Roesta			2 acres	
	do	Heir of Simon Pope			1 acre	
	do	Clement the brewster			1 acre	
	do	William of Stoneye			½ acre	
	do	John the swineherd			½ acre	
	do	Anota atte hythe			1 acre	
	do	– Lovechild			½ acre	
	do	Reginald Kede			1 acre	
1323	Richard Kede	Simon de Keten (freeman)			2 acres	& these, at an inquest concerning land bought by freemen from villeins: Dates:– '6 years ago & 1 year ago'.
1328	Nicholas Rote	Master of Hospital of St John (freeman)			2½ roods	

TABLE XV (continued)

Schedule of Land Transfers

Date*	Description of land	Conditions of holding	First owner	Second owner	Gersuma s	Gersuma d	Heriot s	Heriot d	
11/9/29	F.L., H.L., C, M & 1 acre		William Personn (died)	Juliana, his widow			Horse worth 10/- Part of horse worth 4/-		To hold all as long as she remains unmarried.
11/9/29	H.L. & M		Simon Scut	Philip Scut (son)	10		1	4	See 24/2/28. Same land occupied temporarily by younger brothers of Philip.
	same		Philip Scut	John, son of Geoffrey the smith	30				John to pay Philip 2 qr. wheat, 2 qr. barley, ½ qr. peas & beans pa for life.
	F & 1 acre at Downham Hythe		Geoffrey Scut & wife Roesa	Thomas of Hotham	2				
13/12/29	Land 3 x 2 perches		John Man	Richard (brother) & wife Amicia & their son John	1				
	M & 1 acre & F		John Hayt	John Hayt (son)	2				
4/7/30	Part of C, 16 feet x [?]		John Stot	John Pope & wife Joanna	2				[Much of membrane torn away.] John Stot to hold for life; then land to revert to Pope.
19/7/31	½ acre of demesne	4d pa	Demesne	Hugo Hottele					
	½ acre of demesne	4d pa	Demesne	Robert the smith					
	F.L., M		Simon Cardinal (died)	Hugo Cardinal (son)	40		13	4	Heriot paid in kind (illegible) worth 1 mark.
	F called Nelisdam		Richard Kede	Geoffrey Scut	6				

Land	Rent/value	Holder (from)	Grantee (to)	[membrane] torn	To pay to the lord	Transactions made
5½ acres	1 hen pa	*Thomas Thine* (freeman)	Adam Buk	1	To pay to the lord 1 hen at Christmas.	Transactions made without leave. Revealed by inquest. Adjusted by payment of gersuma.
9¼ acres	[membrane torn]	*not named* (freeman)	Geoffrey Scut	–		
1½ acres	½d pa	do	Geoffrey the smith	3	To pay to the lord ½d at Christmas.	
10/9/31 C		Christiana Bathoke	Hugo Kendale (son)	1	Hugo to give Christiana, for her life, a room in the house, & 2 bushels of wheat & 2 bushels of beans every Michaelmas.	
1 acre 2½ roods		[part membrane missing]	– Columbers	4		
6/3/32 C		– Scut & Joanna his wife	Robert Hasteler	1		
Land 33 x 58 feet, lying nexte to land of her brother Robert 'His land'		Emma Scut	Robert the chaplain	1		
M		William de Stoneye / Simon Dovey (died)	Robert, his son / John, Dovey	3 / 4		Simon had pledged this M to William Brewster who left it to his son Clement to hold for life. As the previous transactions had been illegal (not through the court) the M now went to Simon's son.
Same M		John Dovey	John, son of John Columbers	10		
23/9/32 F.L. & M, H.L., C & 1 acre		Juliana, widow of William Personn (died)	Simon Personn (son)	40 / 20 / 6 / 8		
M	6 marks pa	Robert (chaplain), son of Richard le Keu	Robert son of William Stoneye	3 / 4		Robert the chaplain to continue to hold for life: then land to revert. Robert the chaplain to pay 6 marks pa to Robert Stoneye, on pain of confiscation of oxen & goods.

TABLE XV (continued)

Schedule of Land Transfers

Date*	Description of land	Conditions of holding	First owner	Second owner	Gersuma s d	Heriot s d	
	F called Haseldych	2d pa	do	Simon le Renesson	excused		
2/12/32	H.L., C		Simon, son of Wm. Personn	Henry Personn (brother)	13 4		
	5 acres in fields of Ely		Geoffrey Scut	*Simon de Keten* (freeman)	nil		No gersuma 'because the land was free'.
	5 acres in field of Downham		*Simon de Keten* (freeman)	Geoffrey Scut	nil		Exchange of lands.
	Part of an enclosed yard		William Starling	Robert son of Adam of Chettisham	1		
	Part M, 16 x 16 feet		Reginald Sinerles	Henry Jacob	2		
3/2/33	H.L., M		Adam son of Peter atte hythe (died)	Isabella (daughter)	5	1 4	
	same		Isabella daughter of Adam	Hugo the shepherd & Amicia his wife (see p. 138, 18/6/15)	5		(Amicia was mother of Isabella) To pay rent to Isabella for her life:— 6 bush. wheat, 4 bush. barley, 2 bush. peas & beans pa. If in arrears, Isabella to reoccupy.
	M		Robert son of William de Stoneye	Walter of Stretham & Agnes his wife	3 4		
	6 acres in Binding-land at Apesholt		Agnes Lovechild	John le Scherman	6		
	C & ½ acre over Clayhill		Henry son of William Personn	Simom Personn (brother)			For 10 years from Michaelmas.
5/6/33	⅓ C + 1 rood & ½ H.L.		William Personn	Alicia widow of Richard Kebbe	excused		Transaction was the result of Alicia's claim for dower.
25/9/33	A cottage newly built with an acre of land		Hugh Kendale & Agnes his wife	William de Hothum	Not stated		To hold in villeinage for self & descendants by services & dues.

Date / Description		Grantor	Grantee	No.	Fine	Terms
23/11/33	1½ C (= 1½ ac)	Agnes Rote	John Rote (son)	12		To hold in villeinage for self & heirs by services & dues. John gave his mother a piece of land with a house built on it for her life; John to pay services & dues for it.
	F called The Dam	John Rote	Geoffrey Cardinal	Not stated		To hold in villeinage for self & heirs by services and dues.
11/5/34	3½ roods for 3 croppings	Simon Wareyn	John Dumfrey	6		The 6d was paid 'for the permission'.
31/8/34	C	Peter le Keu (died)	Simon le Keu (son	12		By services & dues. Fealty.
	same	John le Keu	John de Elm	2		For self & heirs by services & dues. Fealty.
28/11/34	¼ F.L., C	Henry Saucer (died)	Alicia his wife	15	¼ horse = 5/-	For duration of her life by services & dues.
	5 perches x 2 perches at D. Hythe	Reginals Sinerles	Ralph le Wright	12		For self & heirs by services & dues. He reserves the right of it.
8/2/35	8d pa — Demesne land 7 ac. 3 roods	Amicia de Stoneye	Nicholas, son of Robert Aleyn	18		To hold at the will of the lord.
30/6/35	7 ac. & M	John Cok	Isabell (daughter)	10		For self & heirs by services & dues.
	same	Isabell, dr. of John Cok	John Cok		½ ox = ½ mark	For his life, by services. At his death to revert to Isabell.
	C & adjacent croft	John Fox	John le Taillour de Ely & Amicia his wife.	2		For selves & heirs by services & dues. He reserves the right of it.
	M	Geoffrey the smith	Emma le Soutere			Messuage was returned having been taken by Geoffrey for seven years. [Emma complained that it was in disrepair but the court found otherwise.] To hold by services.
	C	Robert Aleyn & Isabella his wife & Nicholas their son	Emma (daughter)	12		Robert & Isabella to hold for their lives by services & dues. After their deaths, to revert to Emma & her heirs by services & dues.
20/9/35	F.L. & M	Isabella, widow of Simon Buk	Richard (son)	29		For self & heirs by services & dues. Fealty.

TABLE XV (continued)

Schedule of Land Transfers

Date*	Description of land	Conditions of holding	First owner	Second owner	Gersuma s d	Heriot s d	
16/3/62	H.L., 1½ C		John Rote (incapable)	Robert Rote (son)	Not stated		For self & heirs by services & dues. But Robert to pay 6/- a year to the lord instead of doing the works of the cotland & half cotland, for next four years.
	M		Isabella de Bannesquynne	Thomas Holt	12		For self & heirs by services.
			Reginald Kede				
	F.L. & 10 ac taxable land	do	Richard Buk				
	H.L. & 12 ac	do	Richard le Wright				
	F.L. & 10 ac.	do	Geoffrey Powte				
	F.L. & 8 ac.	do	Hugo le Moy				
	H.L. & 6 ac.	do	John Cook				
	F.L. & 12 ac.	do	John Deye				
	H.L. & 6 ac.	do	John Rote	Vacant lands 'in the hand of the lord'			
	H.L. & 8 ac.	do	Richard le Smyth				
	Q.L.		John Dogit				
	Q.L.		Simon le Smyth				
	C		Richard Dumfrey				
	½ C		Simon Chytom				
	C		John Hayt				
	C		John Docat				
	C		John Deye				
	C		Simon Kede				
	H.L.		Geoffrey de Stoneye				
	'Lands'		Agnes daughter of Robert Atte Welle	Lands confiscated in the lords hand			These two villeins had 'withdrawn' from the manor'.
	'Lands'		John of Ely				

Date	H.L., C	Rent	Simon Kede (deceased)	New tenant		Notes
				Katerina (widow) & Simon Rote her second husband	2	For selves & heirs by services. He did fealty. Change of conditions of tenure: for half land from *per virgam* to rentable with services, for cotland, to pay 4/- pa for 'works'.
6/7/62	Building & croft of 1 acre lying between the holdings of Richard Snow & Thos. de Holt	8d pa for M, 16d pa for croft	Agnes le cook (died at Michaelmas 1361) Building & croft vacant since then (in hand of lord)	John Rote junior & Alicia his wife	40	For selves & heirs by services. They did fealty.
13/9/62	Part of a H.L. = enclosed piece: 4 x 2 perches between the holdings of John Taillour & Wm. Janyn		Richard Buk, but recently vacant, in hand of the lord	John Taillour	6	He took seisin & did fealty.
	Part of H.L. Croft & land, 4¼ acres	4d pa 6/- pa	John Dumfrey Thomas Warner but recently vacant	John Taillour Alicia Page	12 for having time	For 10 years at the will of the lord.
	Piece of land at D. Hythe between the holdings of John Sinerles & John Jacob		Agnes widow of John Bridge	John, son of Ralph the Wright	2 6	For self & heirs by services etc. (This land was formerly belonging to Alicia, daughter of Simon atte hythe.)
5/12/62	2 F = Newdych & Parkditches	40/- pa	In hand of the lord	Thomas Holt		For two years, by dues & services.
8/3/63	1 acre from land of Richard Wright	12d pa	In hand of the lord	William Fish	3 for having time	For six years.
26/6/63	6 acres of demesne	8d pa	Demesne	John Benet of Ely	6 for time	For six years. This land lay above the shepherd's.
	C	3/- pa	John Deye (died June 1361) Land then vacant etc.	Simon atte Townsend	8	To hold for life. This land formerly belonged to Robert Gille.
27/7/63	C, & croft from demesne		John Ducat (d. July 1361) Lands then vacant etc.	John de Kersey, tailor & Amicia his wife	C 12 Croft 20	To hold for their lives by services. They did fealty. (John Ducat had held 'by services 20d a year'.)

TABLE XV (continued)

Schedule of Land Transfers

Date*	Description of land	Conditions of holding	First owner	Second owner	Gersuma s d	Heriot s d	
22/9/63	C		Simon Smyth, but recently vacant	John Veyse	–		For self & heirs by services etc. Fealty. Was elected by whole homage to take the cotland. Provided pledges for maintenance.
	C	4/-pa silver	John Ducat (d. July 1361) Land then vacant etc.	Reginald Brewster & Katerina his wife	10		For their lives. Fealty. (Land lies next to the holding of Katerina Cardinal.)
2/5/65	'Piece of land'		Agnes Bridge	William Deer			This transaction made out of court & not reported by jurors who were amerced 1d each.
	C		John Kendall (then vacant)	Simon Hert	3 for time		For ten years by services etc. Pledge for maintenance.
	H.L., 1½ C & Bakehouse		Robert Rote	Stephen Frost	3 for time		For six years. To pay Robert 40d pa Robert to use it for repairs (pledge).

formerly:
Reginald Kede
Richard son of Simon
John Cok
Richard Wright
John Bridge
John Rote jnr.
John Stoneye
Hugo le Meyre
Simon Sinerles
John Ducat
Richard Wright
Simon Chytom
William Hayt
John Ducat
John Deye
Simon Kede

⎫ Vacant lands

F.L.
F.L.
F.L.
F.L.
H.L.
H.L.
H.L.
Q.L.
Q.L.
2 C
C
C
C
C

Date	Property	From	To	Rent	No.	Notes
17/10/65	Building, 1 acre arable	William, clerk of Ely	Richard Snow		40	Building: next to holding of Richard Snow. Acre of land: between land of Bishop of Ely & land of Simon Hert.
23/4/66	Building	Robert Hunt (per reeve John Wrong)	John Benet of Stretham	8d pa	not stated	Self & heirs by services etc. Fealty. Pledges for maintenance.
	1½ ac of demesne	Alicia Page	Vacant Land	2/- pa		
	Building, croft & 4 ac					
18/9/66	Plot of land	Simon — & Katerina his wife	Simon — / Katerina his wife	6½d pa	2	Surrendered land at 6½d pa. Now held for selves & heirs by services. Fealty. Land was once Adam Elyot's.
7/10/67	H.L.	Reginald Kede, but recently vacant	John Pirde		12	Self & heirs by services etc. Servile fealty.
	6½ ac. of demesne	Demesne	Thomas Amyz, rector	6/6 pa	4 for time	For six years. Land lay next to Rectory.
	1 ac	Richard son of Simon, but recently vacant	John Swift	12d pa	4 for time	To be held at the will of the lord.
	C without a building	William Hayt	Richard Fox	18d pa	6	Self & heirs by services. Fealty. Land once belonged to John Hayt.
	6 ac. of demesne	Demesne	Thomas Holt	6/- pa	4	For ten years. Land lay 'beyond Stakehone'.
2/3/68	A piece of land at D. hythe	William Veel & Agnes (wife)	Robert Moriz & Agnes (wife)			Inquest found that the Veels never had right to this land. It should have gone to Agnes Moriz on the death of her former husband, Simon son of Thomas. Veels in mercy 3d.
26/4/68	M., R.M. 1/3 F	John Bridge (died)	Thomas Bridge son		2	For self & heirs by services. Fealty. Fishery was from Coveney Bridge to Manea.
24/5/68	R.M.	John Hayt, but recently vacant.	Richard Fox		6	Self & heirs by services. Fealty.
	part R.M.	'took from the lord'	Katerina Cardinal	1d pa	8	Self & heirs. Fealty. Lay between R.Ms of William Hayt & Richard Bridge.
	Part F	'took from lord'	Richard Sinerles	2d pa	9	Self & heirs. Fealty. F was part of Dilutredych.

TABLE XV (continued)

Schedule of Land Transfers

Date*	Description of land	Conditions of holding	First owner	Second owner	Gersuma s	Gersuma d	Heriot s	Heriot d	
3/7/68	R.M.	1d pa	Simon Pope, but recently vacant	Wm. Shepherd & Joanna, wife		12			Selves & heirs by services. Fealty. Lay between R.M. of Wm. Hayt & R.M. of Nicholas son of Simon.
	R.M.	1d pa	John Hayt	William Hayt (son)		6			Self & heirs by services. Fealty. Lay between R.M. of Wm. Shepherd & R.M. of Katerina Cardinal.
19/9/68	Part R.M. at D. hythe = 1½ roods		Thomas Bridge	Geoffrey Bridge		18			Self & heirs by services. Fealty. Lay next to R.M. of Geoffrey Bridge.
	1 ac. of F.L. / 1 ac. of Q.L. / 1 ac. of F.L. / 1 ac. of F.L. / ¾ ac. of F.L. / ½ ac. of F.L. / ¼ ac. of demesne / ¼ ac. of C	12d pa	formerly of: Susan Fox / John Ducat / Geoffrey Cardinal / Richard Wright / Nicholas son of Simon / John Cook / Richard Buk / Richard Dumfrey	Vacant lands have been vacant for the past year					
11/5/69	F.L.		John Dumfrey (died)	Vacant land	None because unwilling to take land			ox	Held by services, 14/- pa.
20/9/69	H.L.		John Deye: then vacant	Geoffrey Buk	do				Self & heirs by services. Elected by whole homage to take land. Fealty.
	H.L.		Simon Fox: then vacant	William Hayt	do				Self and heirs by services. Fealty.
	C		John Janyn: then vacant	William Skut	do				do do do
–/12/69	C		Robert Moriz	Simon Chyton		6			For five years. By services & dues. Pledge for maintenance.

150

Date	Holding / land	Rent	Tenant		No.	Notes
4/3/70	Alder grove of ½ ac.		Thomas Bridge	Geoffrey Bridge & Joanna (wife)	40	For selves & heirs by services. Land at D. hythe between holding of Geoffrey Bridge & Downham Common. Fealty.
	F.L. & meadow same	12/- pa 12/- pa	Richard Lacy (withdrew from demesne) Thomas, Rector of Downham	Thomas, Rector of Downham William Skut	43	Rector was pledge for Lacy; & had to take the land. William then took it 'for life', to pay 12/- pa for 12 years: services & dues. Fealty: pledge for maintenance.
29/7/70	1½ ac.	16d pa	John Dumfrey: then vacant	Geoffrey Cardinal		From land of John Dumfrey. To hold by services until another tenant comes to take it.
27/6/73	F.L. F.L. F.L. Q.L. Q.L. H.L. H.L. 2 C C C		formerly: John Cook Richard Wright Richard, son of Simon John Dumfrey Ralph Cardinal John Ducat John Rote Reginald Kede Geoffrey Stoneye Richard Dumfrey Simon Chytom Alice Kynelyn John Ducat	Vacant lands		Proclamation to be made that if any heir or any other who might have right or claim to any of these lands or holdings wishes to demand them he must come to the next court to make his claim.
19/9/73	List same as 27/6/73 except see last column		same as 27/6/73 except see last column	do		Ralph Cardinal's Q.L. replaced by Katerina Cardinal: ¾ L. Proclamation as before.
1/12/73 do	List same as 19/9/73 Also:— *Demesne Corn Land let to tenants* 1 ac. in Myddyl-halle croft 2 ac 1 ac 1¼ ac. 1¼ ac	 12d an acre do do do do	same as 19/9/73 Geoffrey Buk Stephen Becher Robert Rote Alan Draper John Hankyn	do		do For sowing corn. To hold from Michaelmas 1373 for one year. To pay rent at the four usual times of the year in equal parts.

TABLE XV (continued)

Schedule of Land Transfers

Date*	Description of land	Conditions of holding	First owner	Second owner	Gersuma s	Gersuma d	Heriot s	Heriot d	
	2 ac. in Nether-hallecroft	12d pa an acre		William Warner					
	1¼ ac. do	do		William Dunfrey					
	4¾ ac. do	do		John Wrongge					
	11¾ ac. above Barlidonhone	do		John Fysshe, chaplain of Ely					
	40 ac. Warren land above Parkehone	2/- pa an acre		do					
	7½ ac. land over Cornedychone	do		do					
	1¼ ac. over Crouchone	12d pa an acre		John Shephyrd					For sowing corn. To hold from Michaelmas 1373 for one year. To pay rent at the four usual times of the year in equal parts.
	2 ac. do	do		Simon Sinerles					
	2 ac. do	do		William Hayt					
	2 ac. do	do		Thomas Taylour					
	½ ac. do	do		John Taylour					
	1½ ac. over Stake-hone	do		John Walsham					
	4 ac. do	do		Nicholas, son of Simon					
	1 ac. do	do		John, son of Ralph					
	2 ac. do	do		John Curteys					
	2 ac. do	do		John Rote					
	2 ac. over Holm-hone	do		Geoffrey Buk					
	1¾ ac. do	do		John Lovechyld					
4/3/74	*Vacant Lands* as on 19/9/73		same as on 19/9/73	Vacant lands					No claim for lands. Proclamation as before.
do	H.L.	7/- pa	William Janyn (died)	Taken into lord's hand				6	
31/5/74	*Vacant Lands* as on 19/9/73		same as on 19/9/73	Vacant lands					do
21/7/74	do		do	do					do

152

Date	Land	Rent	Tenant	Status	No.	Remarks
	Demesne lands let as on 1/12/73 except as follows: —	12d per acre	Demesne	As on 1/12/73 except as follows: —		As on 1/12/73 except for the reduction of John Fysshe's holding by 25 acres at 2/- an acre.
	11¾ acres	12d an acre		John Fysshe		
	15 acres	2/- an acre		do		
	7½ acres	2/- an acre		do		
do	2 ac. over Chyrchone	12d an acre	Demesne	Stephen Frost	6	To be held for 10 years from Michaelmas 1374.
	2 ac. over Shepehone	8d an acre	do	do	6	do
	M & croft 4¼ ac.	½ mark pa & services	John Swyft	William Parker	12	To hold for life by services.
	M & croft		Richard Snow	Taken into lord's hand		Had been sold without leave (& in disrepair) to John Janyn.
	½ ac. of land		do	do		Had been sold without leave to William Shephyrd.
19/9/74	*Vacant lands* as on 19/9/73		Same as on 19/9/73	Vacant lands		No claim for lands. Proclamation as before.
30/11/75	*Vacant lands* as on 19/9/73		do	Vacant lands		do
13/3/76	¼ rood meadow (demesne)		Geoffrey Cardinal	Taken back into demesne		Had been sold to another tenant without leave.
do	*Vacant lands,* as on 19/9/73 except as shown in Col. 8		As on 19/9/73 except as shown in Col. 8	Vacant lands		Geoffrey Stoneye now omitted from list of vacant lands. No claims. Proclamation as before.
do	Holding		Rosa Stoneye	Taken into lord's hand		Holding dilapidated: no pledge produced.
do	do		John Cook	do		do
do	do; M & 1¼ acres	2/4 pa for services	John Rote (died)	do		No claim yet by heir.
5/7/76	*Vacant lands* as on 13/3/76		As on 13/3/76	Vacant lands		No claims. Proclamation as before.
do	Holding		Rosa Stoneye	Remained in lord's hand		
do	do		John Cook	do		

TABLE XV (continued)

Schedule of Land Transfers

Date*	Description of land	Conditions of holding	First owner	Second owner	Gersuma s d	Heriot s d	
	M & 1¼ ac. croft		John Rote decd. (see 13/3/76)	John Rote, son	Not stated		To hold by services.
	RM, F called Daam, 3½ x 6 perches at D. Hythe		Thomas Bridge	John, son of Richard Sinerles	do		do
	F.L.	14/- pa for services	Richard Wright	see Col. 8			Now to hold H.L. (half of this F.L.) by services & dues by order of the court. The other half at 7/-pa.
	H.L.	by 12/- for services	William Scut	do			Now to hold by services & dues, by order of the court.
24/9/76	*Vacant lands as on 13/3/76*		As on 13/3/76	Vacant lands			No claims. Proclamation as before.
do	Holding		Rosa Stoneye	Remained in lord's hand			
	do		John Cook	do			
	F.L. H.L.		Richard Wright William Scut				Both refused to comply with order of 5/7/76. Distrained against next court.
12/12/76	Holding		John Janyn	Taken into lord's hand			Holding dilapidated: no pledge produced: no chattels.
	Vacant lands as on 13/3/76		As on 13/3/76	Vacant lands			No claims. Proclamation as before.
do	F.L.		Richard Wright	see Col. 8			Ordered by steward to hold H.L. by services & dues. The other H.L. for 7/-pa.
	H.L.		William Scut	do			Ordered by steward to hold by services & dues.

19/2/77	*Vacant lands* as on 13/3/76	Vacant lands	No claims. Proclamation as before.
do	Holding	John Janyn	Remained in lord's hand
17/7/77	*Vacant lands* as on 13/3/76	Vacant lands	No claims. Proclamation as before.

* All in fourteenth century.

F.L. = Full Land   H.L. = Half Land   Q.L. = Quarter Land   M = Messuage   C = Cotland   H = House   R.M. = River Meadow   F = Fishery

TABLE XVI

Yield of Grain per seed (Downham)

Roll	Year	Wheat					Rye					Beans & Peas					Barley					Oats				
		a	b	c	d	e	a	b	c	d	e	a	b	c	d	e	a	b	c	d	e	a	b	c	d	e
2	1318/19	114-0	2½	32-5	93-0	2.85	13-0	2½	4-0	4-7	1.21	53-3	3	20-2	46-6	2.30	23-1	2	6-3	26-1	4.09	23-1	4	10-4	48-7	4.65
4	1321/22	49-0	2½	15-4	34-5	2.23	44-0	nil	nil	nil	nil	19-0	3	16-4	25-1	1.52		3	7-7	28-0	3.55	nil	nil	nil	nil	nil
9	1330/31	71-0	2½	21-0	46-1	2.19	10-0	2½	3-0	8-4½	2.66	32-2	2½	10-1	14-4	1.43	54-1	3½	27-5	86-2	2.64	7-2	4	3-3	3-6	1.11
13	1341/42	54-2	2½	16-6	44-4	2.65	11-2	2½	3-6	0-7 & no more	0.23	37-1	2½	11-6	43-7	3.73	60-2	3½	26-7	94-3	3.51	13-1	4	6-6	10-0	1.48
11	1342/43	55-0	2½	17-5			14-0					33-0	2½	10-4	31-4	3.35	54-0	3½	23-6	97-2	4.09	4-1	4	2-1	3-2	1.52
14	1343/44	65-0	2½	20-5	50-3	2.44	10-0	2½	3-1	8-4	2.72	26-0	2½	8-2	32-5	3.95	53-1	4	25-3	102-3	4.03	8-3	4	4-2	13-2	3.11
15	1344/45	51-0	2½	15-5			12-0	2½	4-1	nil	nil	32-1	2½	10-1	nil	nil	55-0	4	26-7	nil	nil	13-2	4	6-4	nil	nil
17	1345/46	50-0	2½	16-0	27-1	1.69	12-0	2½	4-1	8-2	2.0	34-0	2½	11-0	51-4	4.68	55-0	4	27-1	110-4	4.07	4-2	4	2-2	0-6	0.33
18_1	1346/47	48-2	2½	15-1	48-5	3.21	7-2	2½	2-3	5-2	2.21	28-3	2½	9-0	47-5	5.29	48-2	4	24-2	122-2	5.04	4-2	4	2-2	7-5	3.38
18_2	1347/48	52-0	2½	17-1	42-7	2.50	10.0	2½	3-2	8-3	2.57	43-0	2½	14-2	62-1	4.35	42-0	3	21-1	108-4	5.13	nil	nil	nil	nil	nil
19	1350/51	42-0	2½	13.2	21-7	1.58	9-3	2½	2-6	6-2	2.27	44-2	2½	14-0	31-2	2.23	42-0	4	21-0	75-1	3.57	nil	nil	nil	nil	nil
25	1367/68	52-0	2½	16-0	38-3½	2.39	14-0	2½	nil	nil	nil	14-0	3	5-2	24-1	4.59	32-0	4	16-0	80-1	5.00	15-0	4	7-4	21-0	2.80

a. Acres and roods sown   b. Bushels per acre sown   c. Quarters and bushels sown   d. Quarters and bushels produced   e. Yield per seed

TABLE XVII

Ramsey Yields per seed

	1342	1343	1347	1350
Wheat				
Warboys			5	
Upwood		4		
(Downham)		2.44	2.5	
Oats				
Warboys	6.5			
Upwood		1.5		
Abbots Ripton	2			
(Downham)	1.52	3.11		
Beans and peas				
Warboys			6	
Upwood		3		
Abbots Ripton	1.5			
Weston				1.5
Elton				1
(Downham)	3.25	3.95	4.35	2.23
Barley				
Warboys			8.5	
Upwood		4		
Abbots Ripton	6			
Elton				2
Broughton	2			
(Downham)	4.09	4.03	5.13	3.57

TABLE XVIII

Corn Prices (per quarter of corn)

Roll	Year	Wheat Sold	Wheat Bought	Malt Bought	Malt Sold	Barley Bought	Barley Sold	Rye Bought	Rye Sold	Oats Bought	Oats Sold	Peas & Beans Bought	Peas & Beans Sold	Drage Sold	Drage Bought
1B	1301/02		5/-			6/-	4/4			at 2/6 an acre					
2	1318/19	3/4	4/8,5/4				4/-								
3	1319/20	4/4,4/8							5/-,6/-				4/-		
4	1321/22	13/6	12/-,10/-			8/-	12/-			3/4		2/2 in July			4/-
5	1322/23	10/-	10/-,11/-				8/-						10/-, 8/-, 4/- old, 5/2		
6	1324/25	8/4	7/-			6/6	6/-,6/1 / 5/6	6/-			6/- for fodder				
7	1326/27	3/4,3/6	4/-				3/6	3/6	for sowing	2/3,3/-,2/6	3/6	3/4	5/2	3/4	
8	1328/29	6/3	6/-	4/3 drage malt			4/7½	3/4	for sowing		3/1	3/4	5/2	4/3 for malt	
9	1330/31	6/-,6/8	7/8				4/6		7/8 in grosse		2/8	3/3	4/-,4/4	3/3	
10	1331/32	6/8,7/9	7/10 7/-			6/-	6/8,7/4		6/-	3/-,4/6		5/4	4/-	5/4,6/-	
12	Part 1336/37									for sowing 5/1-	for fodder 2/-				
13	1341/42	4/8	3/7		4/- old		4/-		3/-	1/6,1/8	3/-		for liveries		4/-
11	1342/43	5/8,6/-	4/5½		5/- old		4/-	4/2	4/2	1/-,2/-	3/4				
14	1343/44		4/-		3/-		3/10	4/-	5/-	1/8	3/4				
15	Part 1344/45	2/10							2/-	1/6			2/11		
16	Part 1344/45													2/11	2/11
17	1345/46	for sowing at Swavesey 3/2 in summer & autumn 3/4	3/-			2/6 for sowing	3/-	3/-	2/6 for sowing	1/8,3/-		2/-			2/10
18[1]	1346/47	5/-,6/- in June 5/4 in July					4/4		6/- in April	2/4,2/8 2/8,3/-					
18[2]	1347/48		6/8				4/10 in Dec. 5/- in March			2/4 3/8 3/10,4/- in March					

No.	Year								
18[3]	1348/49	4/4	4/-,4/8		4/- in Nov	4/-		for fodder 2/8 / 1/10,2/-		2/8
19	1350/51	6/8 for familia / 6/-	10/- / 6/-			for sowing 6/-	4/-	3/8	
20	1351/52	6/8,7/8 / 8/-	6/8 old 12/- to the customary tenants		8/- 6/- in Nov		3/5,3/6	6/-	6/-
22	1361/62	for liveries 5/-		6/-					
23	1363/64	5/-,5/8	9/- 7/6		8/-		4/-		
24	1365/66	6/8 at Barnwell	5/4	4/2	4/4 4/-	2/8	3/-,3/4 / 4/-	4/8	
25	1367/68	6/8	7/-	5/4	5/4	4/-	4/-		
26	1368/69	8/- for sowing	9/-	5/4		5/-			
27	1374/75		6/-	4/-					

All prices taken from the Reeves' Money Accounts

Roll	Year	WHEAT				RYE				PEAS &	
		Sold qr. b.	Price per qr.	£ s. d.		Sold qr. b.	Price per qr.	£ s. d.		Sold qr. b.	Pri per
2	1318/19	12-0	3/4	2. 0. 0						6-1½	2/
3	1319/20	{ 30-0 6-4 11-2½	4/5 4/4 4/8	10.13. 8							
4	1321/22	4-4¼	13/6	3. 1. 2		4-5	12/-	2.15. 6		3-7	10
5	1322/23	19-7	10/-	9.18. 9						17-2	8/
6	1324/25	2-4	8/4	1. 1. 0		2-0 2-0	6/- 6/1	1. 4.2¼		25-6 13-7	5/ 4/
7	1326/27	{ 1-7 0-4	3/6 3/4	8.2¾							
8	1328/29	6-0	6/3	1.17. 8						1-5	5/
9	1330/31	{ 2-5 1-5½ 3-0	6/- 6/6 6/8	2. 6.8½		1-0	7/8	7. 8		19-4 1-4½	4/ 4/
10	1331/32	{ 2-2 9-0 7-0 2-0 3-1¾	7/9 6/10 7/- 7/4 6/8	8. 4. ¾		1-0½	6/-	6.4½			
12	pt 36/37					No corn sold					
13	1341/42			none sold		4-3	3/-	13.1½			
11	1342/43	8-3¼	4/8	1.19.2¾		0-7	4/2	3.7¾		7-4	3/
14	1343/44	{ 6-0 5-6¼	6/- 5/8	3. 9.1½		11-7	5/-	2.19.4½		1-0½	3/
15/ 16	part 1344/45	15-0¼	2/10	2. 2. 7		4−5	2/-	9. 3			
17	1345/46					No corn sold					
18¹	1346/47									5-0 5-0	2/ 3/
18²	1347/48	{ 5-0 2-4 9-1	6/- 5/- 5/4	4.11. 2		5-0	6/-	1.10. 0		1-0 17-1 13-0	3/1 3/ 4/
18³	1348/49	5-3½	4/4	1. 3.6¾		4-0	4/-	16. 3ᵃ		20-0	2/
19	1350/51	0-1	6/8	10						0-2	4/
20	1351/52	{ 1-0 1-0	7/8 6/8	7. 8 6. 8		3-1	6/-	18. 9			
22	pt 61/62					No corn sold					
23	1363/64					0.4	8/-	4. 0		5-5	4/
24	1365/66	{ 4-4 25-7	5/8 5/-	7.14. 4		0-4	[4/-]	2. 0		3-0 2-0	3/ 3/
25	1367/68	45-6	6/8	15. 6. 4						8-1	4/
26	1368/69	1-0	8/-	8. 0							
27	1374/75										

Figures taken from the Reeves' money accounts   a, b, c: Reeve's e

Corn

LEY £ s. d. qr.	DRAGE Sold qr. b.	DRAGE Price per qr.	DRAGE £ s. d.	MALT Sold qr. b.	MALT Price per qr.	MALT £ s. d.	TOTAL £ s. d.	Roll
16. 7. 9	13-0	4/-	2.12. 0				21.13. 2	2
1. 6. 6							12. 0. 2	3
			[2.18.9¼]	48-0	10/-	24. 0. 0	34. 4.2¼	4
5.16. 0							22.12. 9	5
16. 6				45-4	7/-	15.18. 6	28. 8.8¾	6
2. 2¼				58-0	4/-	11.12. 0	12. 2. 5	7
		OATS						
5.3¼	6-1½	3/1	19. 4	3-0½ 13-0	4/3 6/-	4.11.0½	8. 1.8¾	8
		DRAGE						
4.10¾	4-0	2/8	10. 8	76-6	7/8	29. 8. 4	37. 9. ¼	9
4. 8. 8	3-1¾ 0-4	6/- 5/4	1. 1.11	39-4	7/-	13.16. 6	27.17. 6	10
								12
				4-0 old	4/-	16. 0	1. 9.1½	13
13.7½							4. 1. 6	11
16.10				50-0 50-0	5/- 4/-	12.10. 0 10. 0. 0	28.18.10¾	14
1. 1.10	4-5½	2/11	13. 8	51-0	3/-	7.13. 0	12. 0. 4	15/16
								17
3.10. 5							4.18. 9	18¹
5. 5.9¾				54-0	6/8	18. 0. 0	35. 8 1½	18²
5. 0. 0				54 1	4/8 4/-	12.16. 0	22. 9.1¾	18³
				66-4	10/-	33. 5. 0	33. 6.10	19
	8-4	6/-	2.11. 0	38-0 3-2	12/- 6/8	23.17. 8	28. 1. 9	20
								22
	14-0	4/8	3. 5. 4	20-2	7/6	7.11.10½	12. 3.8½	23
		OATS						
9. 0. 4	5-4	2/8	14.8	29-2	5/4	5. 8. 0	23.15. 4	24
16. 6. 8	4-0	4/-	16. 0	6-4	7/-	2. 5. 6	36. 7. 0	25
6. 2.10ᶜ	2-4	5/-	12. 6	17-0	9/-	7.13. 0	14.16. 4	26
6				10-0	6/-	3. 0. 0	3. 0. 6	27
							£459. 7. 9¼	

9; (c) £6.2.8.

TABLE XX

Works Due and Sold

Roll	Year	Ploughing works			Summer and winter work			Harvest work			Sold during audit
		Due	Excused†	Sold	Due	Excused†	Sold	Due	Excused†	Sold	
2	1318/19	800			2998	263	849	716	60	228	
3	1319/20	800			3698	296	13	720	59	96*	*+14
4	1321/22	800			3698	219	358	720½	59 + 8	283	
5	1322/23	800		800	3723	218	1948	720½	59 + 6	345½	
6	1324/25	800		800 (at 6d an acre)	3698	226	1761*	686	58	222	*+35
7	1326/27	800			3698	226	1724	696	58 + 6	291	
8	1328/29	800			3698	226	46*	missing	missing	118½	*+238
9	1330/31	800			3618	136½	45½	696		nil	
10	1331/32	800			3718	201½	17½	720½	46½	82½	
12	pt 1336/37	138		138	631½	39	11½*	720½	59	261	*+16
13	1341/42	800		800	3698	225	2672	696	58	638·	
11	1342/43	800		800	3718	228	2680	720½	59	661	
14	1343/44	800		800	3673½	225	2648½	740½	61	679½	
15/16	pt 1344/45	680		680	3146½	193	2273½	237½	19	214½	
17	1345/46	800		800	3763½	225	2672	729	73	656	
18¹	1346/47	780		585	3763½	293½	2638½	708½	70½	638	
18²	1347/48	800		800	missing	missing	2782	missing	missing	686½	
18³	1348/49	800		800	3739	273	2666	733	62½	670½	
19	1350/51	800		519	3718½	245	324	753½	65	*	
20	1351/52	800		illegible	3763½	169½	illegible	730	52	illegible	*+194

†Regular excusals for reeve, hayward and smith; others for infirm tenants.

		Ac	R	Ac	R	Ac	R							
22	pt 1361/62	61 – 2		30 – 3		3 – 1		1482	762		755	393	41*	*+14
23	1363/64	133 – 2		74 – 3		–		4784	2110	373*	892	37 + 405	†	*+33 †+43
24	1365/66	133 – ½		73 – 1½		6 – ½		3784	2423	244	788	452	9	
25	1367/68	136 – 3		73 – 1		14 – ½		3784	2222	466½			60½	
26	1368/69	136 – 3		73 – 1½		9 – 1		3784		516½	774	54 + 400	28½	
27	1374/75	136 – 3		73 – 1		16 – 1		3763	2208	494	753	52 + 389	47*	*+9

INDEX

agriculture, 54–5; acreage, 54, 95, 130; corn prices 158–61; crops 54–5, 93, 130; records, 2, 115; yield, 54, 55, 156, 157
Aldreth Causeway, 13, 15, 17, 93
Amies, Thomas, rector of Downham, 45, 62, **63**, 64, 70
Apesholt, 19, 81
assarts, 18, 19, 94, 95
Balsham, 11
Benet, John, 37, 60
Biggleswade, William of, 42, 44, 67
Black Death, 2, 17, 95; recurrence of, 96
Brewster (Brewer), Clement, 24, 44, 48, 53, 65, 66, 77, 85; John, 38, 44, 48, 49, 73; William, 48, 73
Bridge, family, **75–6**; Agnes, 51; Geoffrey, 61; John, 51; Thomas, 61, 83; William, 51
Bronn, Isabell, 38, 85
Brook, Emma del, 9, 65; Robert del (of the Green, son of Richard le Keu), chaplain, 9, 41, 44, 52, 65, 67, 74, 77, 85, mainpast of, 44, 65
Buk, family, **70–3**; Adam, 14, 41, 52, 60, 61, 68, 84; Agnes (formerly Carpenter), 52; Agnes, d. of Robert, 82; Beatrice (Beaty, Baldy), 8; Geoffrey, 60; John, 60; Simon, 52, 53, 60, 78
Bury St Edmunds, 10, 16
Caldecott, Nicholas de, chaplain, 66, 77
Cambridge, 41, 59
Cardinal, family, **76–9**; Geoffrey, 7, 26, 28, 51, 60, 71, 90; Hugo, 86; Katerina (Katherine), 5, 60, 87; Simon, 26, 41, 42, 43, 51, 52, 60, 65, 67, 68, 71, 85, 90
Carpenter, Warin the, 7, 16
Carter, Robert the, 50
chaplains, 9, **65–6**; *see*: Brook, Robert del; Caldecott, Nicholas
Chatteris, 5, 10
Child, John, 67, 86
Cok, John, 8, 51, 52, 60, 61, 68
Colne (Hunts), 10

Columbers, de (Columbariis), James, rector of Downham, 23, 24, 61, **63**, 64; John, 27, 38, 53, 60, 73, 78, 90; John, son of John, 38, 53
court, 30–47; amercements, 33–34; assize of bread and ale, 8, 28, 29, 34, 37, 116–20; attorneys, 44–5; by-law, 23–9; conveyancing, 46, 47, 124–9, 137–55; fines, 34–5, 47, 90, 124–9; frequency of, 30, 108–14; inquest, 32, 50; jurors, 35, 36, 133–6; location, 30; offences, 37–40; officers, election of, 45, 90; pleas, 41–4; pledges, 32–3; procedure, 31–3, 41–2; records, 2, 39, 108–14; view of frankpledge, 37, 93
Coveney, 5, 75
Coveney Bridge, 5, 75
demesne accounts, 2, 115; arable land, 17, in strips, 4, 82, 89; cultivation, 54, 55, 130; extents, 1, 2, 4, 13–17, 19, 20, 57, leasing of, 18, 87, 88, 94, 96, 97–9, 130 meadows, 5; park, 4; rents, 87, 88, 97–9 131–2; stock, 56–9
dilapidations, 25, 45, 81, 95
Ditton: *see* Fen Ditton
documents, 1–3
Doddington, 5, 10, 11, 40
Dovey, John, 48, 49, 53
dower, 48, 50
DOWNHAM, 4–6; church, 4, 63
common grazing lands, 5, 20, 21
fen, 5, 6, 20–2
fields, 4, 93, 97–9; Acreland, 80, 86, 91 Aggrene (Aggrave), 4, 5, 89; Barleydonehone (Barlidonhone, Barleydon), 71, 77, 97, 99; le Botine, 76, 80, 83, 86, 98; Churchill, 64, 87, 97; Chyrchone, 87; Comedychone, 99; Crouchone, 83, 99; East Field, 4; Gradenedene, 76; Grasshone, 37; Hankele, 73; le Heath, 80, 98; Holm, Holmhone, 72, 78, 81, 87, 88, 89; Middlehallcroft, 72, 99; Netherhallcroft, 99; Parkhone, 99; Parrocesone

164

165

growth of, 19, 94; vacant holdings, 18, 25, 96, 146, 148, 150, 151
Prest, Hugo, 28, 80
Ramsey, 54, 55
Raymund, Earl of Provence, 10
Rote, Caterina, 50, 80; Robert, 8, 81, 87; Simon, 50, 60, 80, 86
Russell, Alice, 50, 52, 73, 74; Robert, 50, 52, 67, 73, 74
St Ives (Hunts), 16
St John of Ely, Hospital of, 13, 14, 30, 66, 77; Masters of, *see* Weston, Thomas de
Sauser, family, **82–3**; Alice, 49; Henry, 49, 68; Simon, 9, 60, 72
Scut, family, **67–70**; Emma, 9, 41, 52, 65; Geoffrey, 14, 49, 52, 60, 61, 66, 73, 79; Nicholas, 9, 49, 52, 61, 65, 77, 80, 82, 89, 90; Philip, 48, 49, 92; William, 18, 60, 64
Shepherd (Chephird), Hugo the, 49, 51, 68, 70, 71, 80, **91**; William, 5, 28, 62, 79, 87
Simon, Nicholas son of, 5, 26, 60
Sinerles, family, **83**; John, 44, 75; Simon, 61
Smith, Geoffrey the, 17, 24, 42, 61, 74, 85, **91**; Jocelyn the, 7, 17; John, 49, 67, 68, 91; Robert the, 8, 53, 71, 77; Rosa, 85, 91
Somersham (Hunts), 10, 11, 16, 57, 59, 80
Souter, Emma le, 42, 91
stock, 56–62; dairy farming, 61; of demesne, 56–9; loss of, 94; plough-team, 57; sheep farming, 59–61, 68, 69, 70, 73, 93; of vill, 59–62
Stonea (Stoneye), 84
Stoneye (de), family, **84–6**; Amicia, 38; Joanna, 82; John, 60, 72; Robert, 38, 52, 91; Rosa, 45, 62; William, 41, 52, 53, 60, 61, 62, 68, 70

Sumencer, John le, 43, 44
Swaffham, William de, rector of Downham, 63
Tailor (Taillour), John, 28, 38
tenurial system, 13–19; customary lands, 14–16, division of, 17, lease of, 17, 18; dues, 16, 17, 47, 124–9; protest against, 18, 70, 96; restrictions, 16, 17; services, 13–16, 93, 94, 95, 96, 162–3; refusal to do, 72, 73, 76, 78, 79, 80, 81, 86, 88, 89, 91, sale of, 94, 95, 96, 162–3
Thine, Thomas, 14, 70
Townesende, Simon atte, 4, 17, 45
transport, 4, 5, 16, 94
vill: by-law, 23, 24; officers of, 24–9, dismissal of, 90, duties of, 25–9, election of, 26, 27, 90, reeve, 24–7, 115
villagers, 7, **63–92**; status of, 7; surnames, 89, 121–2
Wake, Lady Blanche, 10
Walcot, John de, 52, 68
Walsingham, Alan of, 11
Warboys, 55
Warren (Warin), Simon, 70, 86
Well, 41
Welney (Wellenhey), 20
Wereham, John of, 67, 77
Weston, Thomas de, Master of the Hospital of St John of Ely, 52, 68
Wicken Sedge Fen, 20
wills, 52, 67, 71, 73
Wimblington, 20
Winchester, 54, 55
Wisbech, 1, 11, 16, 56, 59
works: *see* tenurial system, services
Wrong, John, 26, 60, 70, 87
Wyset, Roger, 67, 77

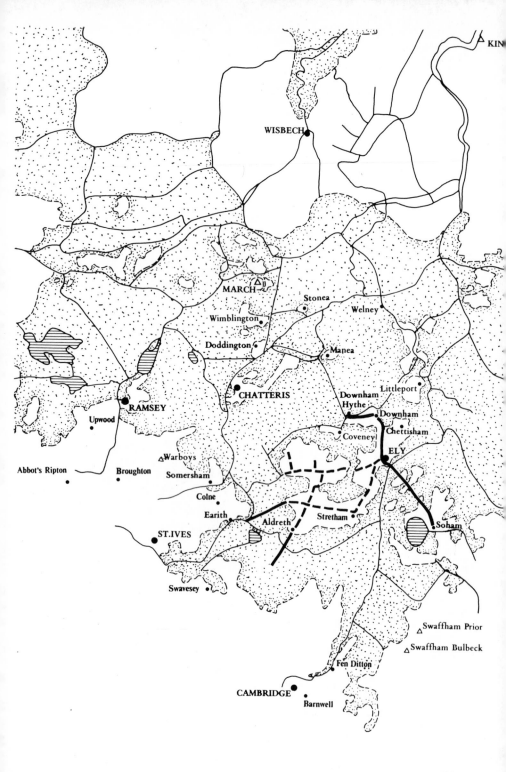